CASE STUDIES

FOR INCLUSIVE SCHOOLS

Second Edition

Peggy L. Anderson

pro·ed
An International Publisher

8700 Shoal Creek Boulevard
Austin, Texas 78757-6897
800/897-3202   Fax 800/397-7633
www.proedinc.com

© 1997, 2005 by PRO-ED, Inc.
8700 Shoal Creek Boulevard
Austin, Texas 78757-6897
800/897-3202   Fax 800/397-7633
www.proedinc.com

All rights reserved. No part of the material protected by this
copyright notice may be reproduced or used in any form or by
any means, electronic or mechanical, including photocopying,
recording, or by any information storage and retrieval system,
without prior written permission of the copyright owner.

Library of Congress Cataloging-in-Publication Data

Anderson, Peggy L.
    Case studies for inclusive schools / Peggy L. Anderson.—2nd ed.
       p. cm.
    Includes bibliographical references.
    ISBN-13: 978-0-89079-991-8 (sc : alk. paper)
    ISBN-10: 0-89079-991-1 (sc : alk. paper)
    1. Mainstreaming in education—United States—Case studies.   2. Children with
disabilities—Education—United States—Case studies.   I. Title.

LC4031.A65 2004
371.9'046—dc22   2004044775

Cover Illustration: Alexandra and Nicholas Kazmierski,
                    Cherry Creek School District, Englewood, CO

Printed in the United States of America

3 4 5 6 7 8 9 10   08

To my students, who are my teachers.

Conservation Note. Most book publishers include what is known as a *half title page.* This page immediately precedes the title page and contains nothing other than the book's title. Including a half title page generally has been PRO-ED's practice as well. In this book, however, we have chosen to eliminate this page. By so doing, PRO-ED has saved the following:

- 125 pounds of paper
- 3 pounds of caustic soda, sulfuric acid, and other chemicals
- 17.5 pounds of coal
- 9.4 gallons of water

CONTENTS

Chapter Four

Emotional/Behavioral Disorders

Chapter Five

Physical Disabilities and Health Impairments

Chapter Six

Communication Disorders

Chapter Seven

Autistic Spectrum Disorders

Chapter Eight

Sensory Impairments

Chapter Nine

Gifted and Talented

PREFACE

The second edition of *Case Studies for Inclusive Schools* provides a major revision of the first edition, but retains the original objective of the book, which is to provide teacher education students with a stimulating format for understanding a variety of inclusion issues in the schools. As my career in higher education has progressed, I have continued to be impressed with the value of case-based teaching. Over the course of teaching both graduate and undergraduate students, I have come to the understanding that my students learn best and enjoy learning most when they are taught through the use of case studies, or "stories." On innumerable occasions, I have watched a sea of glazed expressions turn to heightened interest, and I have listened to the inevitable hush that descends upon the classroom as I begin a retelling of the experiences that I have encountered in my 30-year career in the field. My case studies have allowed me to give life to my teaching. Through the years, I began to write down the stories I observed and put them into different formats for group projects, exam questions, and portfolio artifacts. Student response has always been overwhelmingly positive. It appears my students are fascinated by the problems that occur in real-life situations—and they certainly appear to be much more interested in this content than in their textbooks. I have exploited this interest by making these case studies an integral part of all the classes that I teach. It is my distinct impression that since modifying my courses in this manner, my students not only are much more receptive learners, but they also retain information better because they can relate it to specific experiences.

The second edition of *Case Studies for Inclusive Schools* continues to focus on problem solving from a collaborative perspective. It is my sincere belief that students with disabilities are best served when concerned parties work together to provide them with the most appropriate education possible. Families, teachers, and administrators need to join together to establish a support system that enables a child with disabilities to fulfill his or her potential. As with the first edition, this book does *not* attempt to make any recommendations concerning the best instructional method, placement, or any other course of action with regard to solving specific problems. It was written to encourage teacher education students to explore the different attitudes, problems, and situations that arise in the schools.

The cases that were included in this book were not intended to provide exhaustive coverage of the multitude of different inclusion issues that exist for all children and adolescents with disabilities. They were intended to provide a sampling of problems associated with integrating students with disabilities into general education classrooms with nondisabled peers. Because of the individual differences in children, parents, teachers, and administrators, it would be impossible to develop a compendium of cases covering all the challenges of inclusion and curriculum accessibility in the schools. In the original edition (Anderson, 1997) there were 70 case studies; however, it became apparent soon after publication that this number of cases far exceeded what could reasonably be used in the course of a semester. Colleagues and students alike suggested that the sheer number of cases sometimes appeared to be overwhelming. Thus, in the interest of making the selection process less arduous and furthering the lives of innumerable trees, I have reduced the number of cases to 50. Although this was a difficult undertaking, as few of my colleagues could agree on the particular cases that should be deleted, it was finally accomplished. The content of the case questions was revised to reflect current instructional concerns, which include assistive technology, curriculum accessibility, and standards-based reform issues. The number of case questions was also reduced in the interest of covering the material in a more time-effective manner. The second edition of *Case Studies for Inclusive Schools* represents a streamlined version of the original edition that is more user friendly. Additional features of the revision are described on the following pages.

ACKNOWLEDGMENTS

I am thankful for many colleagues and students who provided assistance in the revision of this book. I am particularly grateful to my colleagues at Metropolitan State College of Denver, who have spent considerable time providing feedback on individual cases and case questions. Dee Warnecke's advice and insight were especially valuable to me in the revision process. Melanie Reid, Lech Wisniewski, and Lisa Altemueller also provided constructive feedback that was integrated into this second edition. My former colleagues at the University of New Orleans, Bill Sharpton and Mary Cronin, have continued to share insightful advice that has shaped the first edition and this revision. Additionally, I am thankful to my many colleagues in the Teacher Education Division of the Council for Exceptional Children, who have provided a variety of suggestions based on their use of the first edition. Very special thanks go to the other individuals who have taught me, year after year, the importance of working with families to achieve inclusion goals.

I would also like to thank my mother, Patricia Carr, who is a longtime veteran special education teacher who holds more disability-area credentials than anyone I know. Beginning many years ago as a teacher of students with visual impairments, she has continued to teach children and adolescents with numerous types of disabilities. In doing so, she has taught me the value of accepting individual differences while holding high expectations for achievement. As I finish this revision, my mother at the age of 76 is still teaching special education at the middle-school level in the Los Angeles public school system.

And finally, I owe gratitude to my husband, Stefan Kazmierski, who provides the support I need to do my work; and to my children, Alexandra and Nicholas Kazmierski, who never seem to tire of listening to my case studies and suggesting creative solutions for increasing inclusive opportunities for children and adolescents with disabilities.

INTRODUCTION

THE CASE STUDY APPROACH

The purpose of this book is to present a sampling of case studies that contain realistic problems for teacher education students to solve. This particular format was chosen because it provides the learner with the opportunity to *apply* information as opposed to merely memorizing it. Historically, case studies have played an important role in the training of many professions and have recently begun to attract increasing attention in the field of education as a means of bringing the role of theory closer to practice (Shulman, 1992). Over a decade ago, the significance of the case study approach was highlighted in the report *A Nation Prepared: Teachers for the 21st Century* (Carnegie Task Force, 1989), which recommended that this teaching method be used as the major focus of instruction for teacher education programs. Goodlad (1990) also supported this recommendation when he suggested that teacher preparation could not be accomplished with "lecture-type courses and with the conventional reading list" (p. 293). There has been a marked increase in the use of case instruction since these recommendations were offered. Today, the use of case studies in teacher preparation programs enjoys considerable popularity and has led to widespread adoption, particularly by those in special education (McNaughton, Hall, & Maccini, 2001). In fact, there are preservice special education programs that offer a case-based curriculum that focuses on teaching content through the use of case methodology (Anderson & Baker, 1999). Similarly, Elksnin (1998) found that 78% of a large sample of teacher trainers in special education were using or had used the case method of instruction, and 17% who had not used it were considering using this strategy in the future. As Andrews (2002) noted, the increasing accumulation of evidence in favor of case-based instruction suggests that most teacher educators are not asking whether cases will be used, but rather *how* they will be used.

The case study format has the distinct advantage of providing the student with the opportunity to better understand the perspectives of others and to make educational decisions based upon a framework of this understanding (Merseth, 1992). As teacher education students, it is sometimes difficult to understand the feelings and attitudes of administrators, parents, and teachers of other specialty areas unless one assumes those particular roles and attempts to advocate for a position other than the one they might necessarily take as teachers. Although videotapes and guest speakers are quite helpful in this case, case studies potentially offer richer opportunities to develop reflection and critical thinking skills among preservice teachers (Tillman, 1995). Another tremendous advantage of using the case study format is the resulting increase in student motivation that accompanies this instructional technique (Shulman, 1992).

Shulman (1992) described four different categories of cases, including case reports, case materials, case studies, and teaching cases. *Case reports* refer to firsthand accounts of experiences, whereas *case materials* refer to raw data used for interpretation of a particular problem. *Case Studies for Inclusive Schools* uses *case studies,* third-person descriptions of a situation, and *teaching cases,* accounts of a particular situation that present a dilemma requiring a solution. These case studies could also be referred to as *case stories* (Ackerman, Maslin-Ostrowski, & Christensen, 1996). They are kept as brief as possible so that the learner has the opportunity to complete a greater number and can benefit from a wider variety of problem-solving situations. As Grossman (1992) suggested, consideration must be given to supplying enough detail to provide the context of the problem at hand, but the restraints of class time for discussion must also be kept in mind.

THE TOPIC OF INCLUSION

The term *inclusion* means different things to different people, although most would agree that it generally refers to the idea of educating learners *with* disabilities in educational settings designed to serve the needs of learners *without* disabilities. Beyond that point, there is considerable disagreement as to exactly what inclusion *does* and *should* mean. As McCarthy (1994) aptly observed, there are few concepts that "are at the same time as attractive and threatening as 'inclusion'" (p. 1). Depending upon one's perspective, the inclusion movement has either promoted the dignity of individuals with disabilities through increased socialization experiences, or it is responsible for demoralizing general education teachers who are not provided the needed support to work with exceptional students and whose classrooms are fast becoming the new "dumping grounds" for special education. Segregation of individuals with disabilities is a recommendation that would find little, if any, support today; however, the determination of the extent of integration is another matter. Whereas in the past, opposition to inclusion may have largely been concerned with the concept itself, today this debate involves the inadequate implementation of inclusive practices (Walther-Thomas, Korinek, McLaughlin, & Williams, 2000).

The standards-based reforms of the 1990s brought new inclusion issues and challenges to the forefront. Concerns regarding accountability for the educational achievement of students with disabilities overshadowed placement issues. Standards-based reformers in large measure interpreted special education in itself to be an insufficient curriculum; these policymakers determined that all students' achievement must address the general education curriculum. Furthermore, it was mandated that students with disabilities must demonstrate this curriculum knowledge in general education assessments. The demands of these new stipulations have resulted in a huge shift of focus in regard to inclusion. Discussions regarding least restrictive environment have been modified to focus on questions regarding curricular issues within the varied environments. Concerns over accessing the general education curriculum have moved to the forefront of discussion (Pugach & Warger, 2001), whereas concerns regarding social acceptance have taken a back seat.

As educators have moved forward to meet the curriculum accessibility challenges imposed by the standards-based reform movement, they have increasingly relied on technology in the inclusive classroom. In 1984, the Center for Applied Special Technology (CAST) was funded with the mission of developing and applying technology in a manner that would expand learning opportunities for students with disabilities (Rose & Meyer, 2002). Although CAST's work originally was devoted to developing technologies that would assist students with disabilities in accessing print media, more recently CAST's efforts have shifted in the direction of using technology in creative ways to transform the nature of the curriculum itself. The standards-based movement and ensuing accountability challenges of inclusive education were influential forces in reshaping CAST's mission and subsequent conceptualization of Universal Design for Learning (UDL). As Rose and Meyer (2002) noted, the central premise of UDL is that curricula should offer alternatives that enhance accessibility for students with different learning styles and disabilities in widely varied settings. UDL offers an instructional lifeline to teachers who are struggling to meet a variety of different learning needs in the inclusive classroom. Similar to the ramps and elevators that are used for alleviating architectural barriers, UDL offers solutions for instructional barriers in the classroom imposed by disabilities. Many of these instructional barriers can be removed through the use of assistive devices. Although the concept of UDL encompasses more than technological innovations, this revision of *Case Studies for Inclusive Schools* specifically addresses the application of technology for solution of instructional problems. Instructors using this book are encouraged to refer their students to Rose and Meyer's (2002) book *Teaching Every Student in the Digital Age,* which is available in full text at the Center for Applied Special Technology (CAST) Web site at http://www.cast.org/teachingeverystudent. In addition to this resource, the CAST Web site offers a wealth of other support for providing assistance to meet the needs of diverse learners in today's classroom.

It is the intention of this book to provide students with an overview of school problems related to inclusion from which they can acquire a better understanding of the multitude of issues that fall under this broad heading. It is *not* the purpose of *Case Studies for Inclusive Schools* to impress upon students that inclusion problems can be unilaterally resolved by promoting one particular viewpoint of integration. The case studies that were included in this book will hopefully lead students to the understanding that there can be no single recommendation for an educational placement, remedial program, or assistive device that would be optimal for all children and adolescents with disabilities. Each learner with a disability will have different needs; these needs must be addressed from the perspective of individuality rather than from the notion that there is one answer that is equally suited to all.

ORGANIZATION OF THE BOOK

The revised edition of *Case Studies for Inclusive Schools* uses the traditional categorical approach to describing disabilities as originally delineated in the Education for All Handicapped Children Act of 1975 (P.L. 94-142) and modified in the Individuals with Disabilities Education Act of 1990 (IDEA) and subsequent reauthorizations. In the original edition, a "needs-based" approach was used to organize the material for each chapter. Although this was considered to be a preferable approach because it focused on the needs of the individual with the disability, the structure ultimately created some confusion on the part of users. Although the classification of individuals on the basis of special education category appears to be an artificial conceptualization that engenders stereotypical notions of a particular disability, it can also promote better communication regarding the nature of the disability for the provision of services. For example, in the first edition of *Case Studies for Inclusive Schools,* the cases that addressed emotional disturbance were included in the chapter entitled "Affective Needs," which is the Colorado needs-based category for serving children and adolescents with this type of disability (Swize, 1993). Unfortunately, the term *affective needs* caused a certain amount of confusion, as many colleagues and students alike were unsure of the meaning of this term. The same was true for the chapter entitled "Cognitive and Adaptive Needs," which addressed children and adolescents with mental retardation. Unarguably, most special educators believe in the value of focusing on the needs of students with disabilities instead of the labels, yet in some cases there is value for the sake of communication in using a categorical system.

COLLABORATIVE PROBLEM-SOLVING EMPHASIS

Throughout the case studies included in this book, the intended focus is on the importance of individuals working together to generate solutions for problems in school settings. It is *not* the intention of this book to cast blame on certain individuals for holding viewpoints that are inconsistent with the goals of inclusion or to criticize those individuals for their viewpoints. On a prima facie level, certain attitudes may appear to be discriminatory, but often they are based more on ignorance than on any prejudicial feeling or any conscious desire to exclude individuals from the mainstream of the community. A careful examination of these attitudes within a problem-solving perspective often facilitates new understanding and acceptance of a different point of view.

USE OF THE BOOK

Case Studies for Inclusive Schools is intended to be used as a supplementary text for introductory courses in special education. It is also recommended for use with online special education courses and school district in-services. This book was written to be used in two different ways: (a) in small-group activities during class time and (b) as individual activities to be completed before or after class for the purpose of discussion or evaluation of course content knowledge. It should be noted that the case study activities cannot be satisfactorily completed without referring to other resources, such as the course text or internet

Web sites. Students must understand that case solutions should be based on opinion that has a legitimate foundation. For example, it would not be sufficient for a student to recommend a certain solution for a child in question merely because of the student's feelings concerning the issue. The student would need to make the recommendation based on specific information in the book or other literature. Given that understanding, varying solutions should be encouraged and received in a manner that encourages diversity in problem solving. The following explanation provides recommendations for case study uses.

 ## Matrix

The matrix of cases, organized by level of intervention, is provided as a quick reference for selecting cases according to topical issues. Revisions in the matrix include the addition of assistive technology as a category and the expansion of coverage in the area of transition to address the needs for these supports at all levels of schooling.

Small-Group Activities

When this book is used for small-group activities during class, it is recommended that the first portion of the class be devoted to the case study content (e.g., learning disabilities). The second portion of the class should then focus on the case study problem-solving activity to provide further understanding of difficulties encountered by children and adolescents with academic and language needs. It is also suggested that the small groups be formed according to the level of teacher preparation—that is, early childhood, elementary, or high school—in order to make the activity more relevant to the students. Most introductory special education classes are designed for all preparation levels. Use of this case study book allows students the opportunity to better understand issues that are related to developmental and educational levels. The problems that accompany inclusion at the kindergarten level are vastly different from those confronted at the 10th-grade level.

There are two types of case study activities that can be accomplished in small-group settings. The first type of activity is *role playing,* in which the group members are asked to assume various roles and then reach a solution for the problem described in the case study. This kind of activity should produce a lively discussion that culminates in a resolution agreed upon by all participants. Students are then asked to summarize in writing the results of this problem-solving effort so they can refer to it later for study purposes. After the small-group activity, it is helpful for the entire class to listen to these summaries so they can be exposed to the different types of resolutions generated by the individual groups. In the revised edition of *Case Studies for Inclusive Schools,* many of the original role-playing activities were deleted in the interest of reducing the length of the book. However, there are six role-playing activities included in this edition. For instructors who choose to do more role playing, practically any case could be chosen from which individual roles and task solutions could be assigned.

The second type of small-group activity is the *group case analysis,* which requires the students to answer questions about the problem presented in the case study. In order for this case analysis to be effective, the group must discuss each question and attempt to reach a consensus of opinion with regard to the issues at hand. It is not effective for the individuals to answer each question on their own and then discuss the answers when everyone has finished. The group as a whole must work through the questions in a collaborative manner, which is not unlike the process that occurs in the schools. If after doing this an agreement cannot be reached, then the group should make a note of this fact and go on to the next question.

Individual Activities

There are two types of individual activities in this book. One type of individual activity focuses on answering the questions following each case study. This activity is designated as *individual or group case analysis.* The group method of problem solving was discussed earlier. Although there are definite advantages to group problem solving, one disadvantage concerns class time. There is usually not sufficient class time to cover the number of cases necessary to give students an appropriate overview of the complexity of problems that can occur in school settings. For this reason, it is recommended that students be assigned various case studies to complete outside of class. The individual case analysis is also recommended when this book is used as a resource for an online course. The completed work can then be discussed in class, or it can be turned in to be evaluated by the instructor. Although there are some knowledge-level questions included in these case analyses, for most of the questions that are raised there are no right or wrong answers. Students can demonstrate their ability to apply course content by adequately supporting their opinions with facts, such as legal precedents and recommendations from literature focusing on that particular topic. When these arguments are presented in a logical and thoughtful manner and in clear narrative writing, students should receive a passing grade.

The other individual activity included in this case study book involves the use of a narrative writing assignment in which the student is asked to provide a detailed analysis of a case. This activity is referred to as an *individual learning plan* that requires the student to identify and address specific problems by developing an educational plan to meet the student's needs. This activity can be used as a work sample for the course or as an artifact for a teacher education portfolio.

Questions

Questions have been revised to reflect the current trends in the public schools today. Standards-based instruction, increased use of assistive devices, and the growing need for transition services at all levels have been addressed in these questions. Although social issues continue to be important for encouraging acceptance of individuals with disabilities, students in teacher education need to understand that the pressures of meeting curricular benchmarks will be the major challenge for the duration of this decade.

In this revised edition, the number of questions was cut to five per case in an effort to reduce the amount of time required to cover each case study. For those instructors who find that the five questions do not provide adequate coverage of topics, a sixth question denoted as "Create A Question" can be added. Instructors can develop an additional question that is deemed relevant to the instruction of a unit or the instructor can ask the students to develop and answer a sixth question that pertains to a case issue that the student chooses to explore in greater depth. This Create-A-Question feature should be viewed as optional.

CREATE-A-QUESTION EXAMPLES

1. Explain how to adapt a fifth-grade science lesson to meet the needs of this student.

2. Write four long-term goals for this student's IEP.

3. Identify four Web sites that could be used to meet the needs of this student and explain why each would be helpful.

4. Identify four transition goals that should be included in this student's IEP.

5. Explain what tests and other types of measurement should have been included in this student's special education evaluation.

6. How could Universal Design for Learning (UDL) strategies be implemented to enhance the achievement of this student?

RECOMMENDED WEB SITES FOR CASE STUDY QUESTIONS

The following Web sites may be useful for assisting students in answering the case study questions. Most of these are general special education Web sites, but a few of them are devoted to specific disability areas. Students who use these sites should be encouraged to reference them in their case study solutions.

http://www.ideapractices.org/
Idea Practices. This is a Web site designed to answer questions about the Individuals with Disabilities Education Act and to provide information about special education services.

http://www.cec.sped.org/
The Council for Exceptional Children (CEC). This is the official Web site for the largest international professional organization dedicated to improving educational outcomes for individuals with exceptionalities.

http://www.eric.ed.gov/
Educational Resources Information Center. This is a centralized bibliographic database of journal articles and other published and unpublished education materials.

http://seriweb.com/
Special Education Resources on the Internet. This is a collection of online special education resources.

http://www.specialednews.com/
Special Education News. This is a Web site that features publications focusing on special education news for teachers and families.

http://www.nichcy.org/
National Dissemination Center for Children with Disabilities. This is a central source of information for IDEA, No Child Left Behind, and educational research practices.

http://www.disabilityresources.org/
Disability Resources Monthly Guide. This site provides a wealth of information related to disability issues that promotes awareness of the needs of individuals with disabilities.

http://www.ldonline.org/
LdonLine. This is a WETA-sponsored Web site that focuses on learning disabilities for parents, teachers, and other professionals.

http://www.ldanatl.org/

Learning Disabilities Association of America. This is the official Web site for the largest professional organization devoted to learning disabilities.

http://www.interdys.org/index.jsp

International Dyslexia Association. This Web site provides information for meeting the needs of students with reading disabilities.

http://clerccenter.gallaudet.edu/

Laurent Clerc National Deaf Education Center of Gallaudet University. This site provides information, curricula, instructional techniques, and strategies for students who are deaf and hard of hearing.

http://www.chadd.org/

Children and Adults with Attention Deficit/Hyperactivity Disorder. This site provides resources for assisting students with attentional deficits.

http://www.neuro.pmr.vcu.edu/

National Resource Center for Traumatic Brain Injury. This site provides information to assist parents and professionals working with students with brain injuries.

http://www.conductdisorders.com/

Conduct Disorders.com—A Soft Place to Land. This site provides information related to meeting the needs of children and adolescents with a wide variety of behavioral difficulties associated with autism spectrum disorders, attention deficit disorder, and emotional disorders.

http://www.nimh.nih.gov/

National Institute of Mental Health. This site provides resources for addressing the needs of individuals with mental illness.

http://www.kn.pacbell.com/wired/bluewebn/

Knowledge Network Explorer: Blue Web'n. This site provides a library of creative lesson plans for meeting the instructional needs of learners at all levels of achievement.

http://www.cast.org/

Center for Applied Special Technology. This site provides resources for using technology and other strategies to access learning opportunities for students with disabilities.

http://www.aamr.org/

American Association on Mental Retardation. This site provides information for addressing the needs of individuals with mental retardation.

MATRIX OF CASE STUDIES

Early Childhood and Primary Level

	Age	Assessment	Instructional	Legal	Collaboration	Transition	Placement	Cultural	Assistive Tech
Antonio	7		X		X		X		X
Susanne	5	X	X		X	X	X		X
Eli	7		X		X	X	X		X
Lemar	6		X		X	X	X	X	X
Sammy	8	X	X	X	X			X	X
Casey	8	X	X	X	X		X		X
Joseph	6		X		X	X			X
Levonda	6		X		X	X	X		X
Rinna	5		X		X	X	X		
Nicole	5	X	X	X	X	X	X		X
Travis	4		X	X	X	X	X		
Kayla	4		X		X	X	X	X	X
Brenna	6		X	X	X	X	X		X
Ted	6		X		X	X	X		X
Lily	5		X	X	X		X		

(continues)

Elementary

	Age	Assessment	Instructional	Legal	Collaboration	Transition	Placement	Cultural	Assistive Tech
Jessie	8		X		X		X		X
Juan	10	X	X		X			X	X
Kevin	11	X	X		X	X	X		X
Elizabeth	10		X		X				X
Hwa-Fang	9	X	X	X	X	X	X	X	X
Jason	10		X		X		X		X
Maria	9	X	X		X				
Jody	9		X		X		X	X	
Miguel	10		X				X	X	
Mitchell	11		X	X	X		X		
Janell	10		X		X		X		
Richard	9	X	X				X	X	
Veru	10		X		X		X		X
Emilio	9	X	X		X		X	X	X
Valerie	10		X	X	X		X		X
Jeffrey	8		X		X		X		X
Arletha	10	X	X		X		X	X	

(continues)

Middle/High School

	Age	Assessment	Instructional	Legal	Collaboration	Transition	Placement	Cultural	Assistive Tech
Aaron	17		X		X	X			
Marta	18	X	X	X	X	X	X		X
Vincent	18	X	X		X	X	X		
David	13		X		X		X		X
LeShawn	15		X	X	X	X		X	X
Joel	17		X	X	X				
Chad	12		X		X				
Melissa	13		X	X	X	X			
Robert	16		X	X	X	X	X		X
Mark	12		X		X	X	X		
Yuri	16	X	X		X		X	X	X
Greg	13	X	X	X	X	X	X		
Paul	16	X	X		X	X	X	X	
Jake	14		X		X	X	X	X	
Karen	17		X		X		X		X
Lauren	13	X	X	X	X	X		X	X
Leo	15		X		X	X	X		X
Margo	14		X		X				

REFERENCES

Ackerman, R., Maslin-Ostrowski, P., & Christensen, C. (1996). Case stories: Telling tales about schools. *Educational Leadership, 53*(6), 21–23.

Anderson, P. L. (1997). *Case studies for inclusive schools.* Austin, TX: PRO-ED.

Anderson, P. L., & Baker, B. K. (1999). A case-based curriculum approach to special education teacher preparation. *Teacher Education and Special Education, 22,* 188–192.

Andrews, L. (2002). Preparing general education pre-service teachers for inclusion: Web-enhanced case-based instruction. *Journal of Special Education Technology, 17*(3), 27–35.

Carnegie Task Force on Teaching as a Profession. (1989). *A nation prepared: Teachers for the 21st century.* New York: Carnegie Forum on Education and the Economy, Carnegie Corporation.

Education for All Handicapped Children Act of 1975, 20 U.S.C. § 1400 *et seq.*

Elksnin, L. K. (1998). Use of the case method of instruction in special education teacher preparation programs: A preliminary investigation. *Teacher Education and Special Education, 21,* 95–108.

Goodlad, J. I. (1990). *Teachers for our nation's schools.* San Francisco: Jossey-Bass.

Grossman, P. L. (1992). Teaching and learning with cases: Unanswered questions. In J. H. Shulman (Ed.), *Case methods in teacher education* (pp. 227–239). New York: Teachers College Press.

Individuals with Disabilities Education Act of 1990, 20 U.S.C. § 1400 *et seq.*

McCarthy, M. (1994). Inclusion and the law: Recent judicial developments. *Research Bulletin, 13,* 1.

McNaughton, D., Hall, T. E., & Maccini, P. (2001). Case-based instruction in special education teacher preparation: Practices and concerns of teacher educator/researchers. *Teacher Education and Special Education, 24,* 84–94.

Merseth, K. (1992). Cases for decision making in teacher education. In J. H. Shulman (Ed.), *Case methods in teacher education* (pp. 50–63). New York: Teachers College Press.

Pugach, M. C., & Warger, C. L. (2001). Curriculum matters: Raising expectations for students with disabilities. *Remedial and Special Education, 22,* 194–196.

Raven, J. C., Court, J. H., & Raven, J. (1986). *Raven's Progressive Matrices.* London: Lewis.

Rose, D. H., & Meyer, A. (2002). *Teaching every student in the digital age: Universal design for learning.* Alexandria, VA: Association for Supervision and Curriculum Development.

Shulman, L. S. (1992). Toward a pedagogy of cases. In J. H. Shulman (Ed.), *Case methods in teacher education* (pp. 1–30). New York: Teachers College Press.

Sparrow, S. S., Balla, D. A., & Cicchetti, D. V. (1984). *Vineland Adaptive Behavior Scales.* Circle Pines, MN: American Guidance.

Swize, M. (1993). Colorado's Needs Based Model. In Colorado Department of Special Education (Ed.), *Instructionally differentiated programming: A needs based approach for students with behavior disorders* (pp. 6–13). Denver: Colorado Department of Education.

Thorndike, R. L., Hagen, E. P., & Sattler, J. M. (1986). *Stanford-Binet Intelligence Scale* (4th ed.). Chicago: Riverside.

Tillman, B. (1995). Reflections on case method teaching. *Action in Teacher Education, 17*(1), 1–8.

Walther-Thomas, C., Korinek, L., McLaughlin, V., & Williams, B. (2000). *Collaboration for inclusive education: Developing successful programs.* Needham Heights, MA: Allyn & Bacon.

Wechsler, D. (1967). *Wechsler Preschool and Primary Scale of Intelligence.* San Antonio, TX: The Psychological Corp.

Wechsler, D. (1991). *Wechsler Intelligence Scale for Children–Third Edition.* San Antonio, TX: The Psychological Corp.

CHAPTER 1

Learning Disabilities

Aaron

Aaron is a 17-year-old senior at Chatsworth Senior High School where he is currently enrolled in the life skills program. This is a transition program designed to meet the career and community living goals of students with disabilities. These students spend their mornings at the school learning functional skills and their afternoons working on a job in the community. Aaron has spent the last 3 months working at a family business where he was eventually to be employed on a full-time basis when he finished school at Chatsworth. Aaron's father and his partner have owned this machine parts business for 20 years.

Yesterday, Aaron's father, Mr. Martinson, came in to see Mr. Larriva, who is Aaron's life skills teacher, and Mr. Fahey, who is Aaron's vocational counselor. Mr. Martinson was extremely upset, almost to the point of being tearful. After 3 months of having Aaron work part time at his machine parts store, he has discovered that his son does not have the skills necessary to keep this entry-level position in the business. His partner of 20 years has asked him to fire Aaron, and Mr. Martinson knows his partner is right. Included in the long list of Aaron's job problems were complaints about his inability to follow directions, inability to organize, and lack of motivation. One example of organizational problems was related to his responsibilities in the warehouse. When Aaron was asked to clean up the warehouse, he would go inside, pick up any loose parts, and then put them in whatever box happened to be nearby. Consequently, different machine parts were being mixed together, causing major problems with orders. When his attention was called to this problem, Aaron did not seem to see that the parts looked different and, therefore, should not be in the same box.

Mr. Martinson talked at length about other problems with organization and misuse of time. For example, on one occasion Aaron was asked to take all the orange-colored files out of the file cabinets and place them in a separate box. Instead of pulling out only the orange files, Aaron took all the files out of each drawer and spread them around on the office floor. Mr. Martinson was astonished when he walked into the office and saw the mess. Aaron was perplexed by his father's reaction because he felt he was doing a more thorough job this way. However, when Aaron tried to put the current files back into the cabinet in alphabetical order, he found that he could not. He became so frustrated that he dropped the task and went on to something else back in the warehouse. Mr. Martinson had his secretary clean up the filing mess because he did not want his partner to see it. According to Mr. Martinson, the worst part of the whole situation is that Aaron does not even seem to recognize when he does something wrong, nor does he show any desire to improve or to learn from his mistakes. Since Aaron has come to work, Mr. Martinson has felt that he does nothing all day except put out fires.

The whole experience has caused significant despair for Mr. Martinson. As he told Mr. Larriva and Mr. Fahey, "If my son doesn't have the skills to work for me in this type of job, what can he do?" He also told the teachers that he does not even understand what a learning disability is or whether it can be cured. It was his understanding that Aaron would always have problems in school, but no one ever told him that Aaron wouldn't be able to hold down a job. Mr. Martinson asked the teachers if there was anything he could do to help his son.

Background Information:

Aaron was diagnosed as having a learning disability in the third grade. The special education evaluation report indicated that Aaron had a receptive language weakness, which was manifested in difficulty following directions. A reading disability, a lack of visual–motor coordination, and attentional deficits were also identified. Aaron was placed in a self-contained learning disabilities classroom from the fourth grade to the sixth grade. During middle school, he attended a resource program where he received help for 50 minutes each day. For the first 3 years of high school, he was placed into low-ability classes where he received supplementary help from special education teachers on a tutorial basis. Aaron was considered to be an ideal candidate for the life skills program.

Aaron's special education teachers always felt that he was a hard worker; however, that evaluation was not shared by some of his general education teachers who described him as "lazy, inattentive, disorganized, and unmotivated," among other things. His parents provided him with a good deal of support. Records indicated that both Mr. and Mrs. Martinson

© 2005 by PRO-ED, Inc. All rights reserved. Duplicating this page is strictly prohibited.

CASE STUDIES

were present at the initial staffing and at every annual review conference for the past 8 years.

Aaron has enjoyed the life skills program at Chatsworth, and he has expressed a great deal of satisfaction in "working for my dad." Both Mr. Fahey and Mr. Larriva are surprised that things are not going well at the machine parts business. On the occasions that Mr. Fahey visited the site, he had the impression that Aaron was working hard. Aaron has the impression that his services are greatly needed at his father's business. He has mentioned on several occasions that he wants to hurry and graduate from the life skills program so that he can help out full time at the parts business.

 ## Case Study Activity

Individual or Group Case Analysis

Answer the following questions and be prepared to discuss them in class.

1. How is it possible that Mr. Martinson has attended all of those school meetings over the course of 9 years and yet does not understand his son's learning disability? How might this misunderstanding have been avoided?

_____

_____

_____

_____

_____

_____

_____

2. Do you believe that Aaron has motivation problems? Why or why not?

_____

_____

_____

_____

_____

_____

_____

© 2005 by PRO-ED, Inc. All rights reserved. Duplicating this page is strictly prohibited.

3. Why do you think Aaron's special education teachers saw him in a different light than his general education teachers?

_____

_____

_____

_____

_____

4. Which of the problems identified in Aaron's original special education evaluation may be interfering with his job performance at the machine parts business?

_____

_____

_____

_____

_____

5. What could Mr. Larriva and Mr. Fahey do to assist Aaron in this situation? What can they do to help this family?

_____

_____

_____

_____

_____

6. Create A Question (optional)

_____

_____

_____

_____

_____

© 2005 by PRO-ED, Inc. All rights reserved. Duplicating this page is strictly prohibited.

CASE STUDIES

Antonio

Antonio is a 7-year-old first-grade student at Costilla Elementary School. Last year, in kindergarten, he was diagnosed with Tourette's syndrome. Antonio exhibits complex vocal and motor tics. In terms of his vocal tic behaviors, Antonio makes animal sounds, spits, belches, and hums. Other tic behaviors include sticking out his tongue, sucking his thumb, poking, and pinching. Antonio also demonstrates coprolalia (the uncontrolled use of obscene language). He has poor language skills, with his expressive language being placed at the 4-year-old level and his receptive language at the 5-year-old level. Antonio has limited readiness skills. He does not consistently identify letters or numbers, and he has a very difficult time with visual–motor skills, such as cutting and writing. He also has poor attention skills and some degree of impulsivity.

Background Information:

Antonio had a very difficult time in kindergarten. His vocal and motor tics interfered with classroom expectations to the extent that the school nurse was assigned full care of Antonio for the $2\frac{1}{2}$ hours of kinder-

garten. (The school did not have funds available to hire an aide for this class.) He was referred for evaluation during the first week of school. This evaluation concluded that Antonio had Tourette's syndrome as well as learning disabilities. Because the psychologist and the kindergarten teacher, Mrs. Vigil, viewed the behavior associated with Tourette's as the primary disability, it was recommended that Antonio be placed in a special school that serves children with severe emotional disturbances. The parents declined special school placement because they lived right across the street from Costilla Elementary, and they wanted Antonio to go to the same school as his three siblings. Mrs. Vigil held the opinion that Antonio could refrain from the tic behaviors if he chose to do so. She frequently punished him for these tics. For example, any vocal tics that she considered to be disruptive to the class were identified as good cause for an extended time-out in the office. Although they were very unhappy with Mrs. Vigil's treatment of Antonio, the parents felt that he should be in his neighborhood school. They are hopeful that Antonio will have a better experience in Mrs. Selby's first-grade class.

Case Study Activity

Individual or Group Case Analysis

Answer the following questions and be prepared to discuss them in class.

1. What is Tourette's syndrome? Is it typical for a child with Tourette's to also have learning disabilities and attentional problems?

_____

_____

_____

_____

_____

© 2005 by PRO-ED, Inc. All rights reserved. Duplicating this page is strictly prohibited.

2. What can Mrs. Selby do about Antonio's tic behaviors? Give four specific suggestions.

_____

_____

_____

_____

_____

_____

3. Do you think a general education setting is more appropriate than the special school for students with emotional disturbances that was recommended following Antonio's evaluation? Do you think Antonio's kindergarten program was appropriate?

_____

_____

_____

_____

_____

_____

4. If you were Mrs. Selby, what specific strategies would you use to increase Antonio's visual–motor skills? Give four specific strategies.

_____

_____

_____

_____

_____

_____

© 2005 by PRO-ED, Inc. All rights reserved. Duplicating this page is strictly prohibited.

CASE STUDIES

5. How could Mrs. Selby use assistive technology to meet Antonio's needs? Identify at least two types of technology that could be used and explain why these might be effective.

_____

_____

_____

_____

_____

_____

_____

6. Create A Question (optional)

_____

_____

_____

_____

_____

_____

_____

_____

Jessie

Jessie is an 8-year-old third grader at Eastlake Elementary. He was diagnosed with a learning disability at the age of 7. Jessie is in Mr. Stewart's third-grade class for a full instructional day, and he receives the help of a special education teacher, Mrs. Panno, for 50 minutes per day. Mr. Stewart and Mrs. Panno are currently in the process of planning Jessie's language arts program.

Background Information:
Jessie's first-grade teacher referred him for special education evaluation. She was concerned because he could not identify letters or basic geometric shapes. Additionally, he seemed to have difficulty learning sounds in the beginning phonics program. The pupil assessment team determined that Jessie had normal intellectual potential (IQ of 115) but significant deficits in both visual and auditory perception. In spite of these deficits, Jessie's vocabulary and comprehension of connected language were well above expectancy for a child of his age. Although the assessment team identified a learning disability at this time, Jessie's parents, Mr. and Mrs. Wagner, refused special education placement. They felt that because Jessie was

© 2005 by PRO-ED, Inc. All rights reserved. Duplicating this page is strictly prohibited.

such a bright child with good verbal skills, they did not want to label him with a problem that might eventually take care of itself. They believed that given additional time to develop, Jessie would catch up with his first-grade peers.

By the middle of Jessie's second-grade year, he still had made little progress. Although he could identify letters, he could not consistently recognize any of the vocabulary that his peers read, nor could he put any sounds together with letters to consistently create appropriate phoneme–grapheme correspondences. Mr. and Mrs. Wagner reconsidered his educational curriculum and asked that he receive special education services starting in the third grade.

Case Study Activity

Individual or Group Case Analysis

Answer the following questions and be prepared to discuss them in class.

1. Would a multisensory reading approach be beneficial for Jessie? Why or why not?

_____

_____

_____

_____

_____

_____

2. Now that Jessie is receiving special education services, do you think he will be able to make normal progress in reading?

_____

_____

_____

_____

_____

_____

© 2005 by PRO-ED, Inc. All rights reserved. Duplicating this page is strictly prohibited.

CASE STUDIES

3. Would it be a good idea for Jessie to be pulled out of his third-grade class to receive intensive reading instruction, or should Mrs. Panno work with him in Mr. Stewart's class on the standards-based curriculum with his third grade peers? Give three reasons for your answer.

_____

_____

_____

_____

_____

_____

_____

4. Should Jessie have started special education services in the first grade? Can you explain why Mr. and Mrs. Wagner felt it would be better for Jessie not to be identified as a special needs child? Is it possible that learning problems can be alleviated with additional maturity?

_____

_____

_____

_____

_____

_____

_____

5. How could assistive technology be used to support Jessie's remedial reading program? Identify two technological devices and explain how these would be beneficial in teaching reading to Jessie.

_____

_____

_____

_____

_____

_____

_____

© 2005 by PRO-ED, Inc. All rights reserved. Duplicating this page is strictly prohibited.

6. Create A Question (optional)

_____

_____

_____

_____

_____

_____

Juan

Juan is a 10-year-old third grader at Villano Elementary School. He is a bilingual child who was recently placed in special education. Juan is considered to be Spanish dominant for receptive language but English dominant for expressive language. He was tested in both Spanish and English for the special education evaluation. His *Wechsler Intelligence Scale for Children–Third Edition* (WISC–III; Wechsler, 1991) profile indicated that his verbal IQ was 82, while his performance IQ was 74. Academic testing revealed a reading disability. Juan is currently reading on a second-grade level in English, and his Spanish reading is at approximately the same level. Although Juan demonstrated knowledge of word attack skills, his sight word vocabulary was considerably lower because of numerous reversals in his reading. His math skills appear to be somewhat higher, at approximately the early third-grade level. Other areas of weakness that were noted in the testing were illegible handwriting and poor eye–hand coordination.

At the staffing, Juan's teachers from the previous year commented on some of his problems in the classroom. Juan's reading teacher, Ms. Renfro, felt that many of his reading problems were due to visual confusion; he frequently reversed both letters and words. His second-grade teacher, Mrs. Fernandez, noted that he had a very difficult time with any board work. She said that he could not copy accurately from the board. She noted that his handwriting was so poor that it was difficult to evaluate his written work. Mrs. Fernandez also expressed concern regarding Juan's socialization. She identified him as a loner who did not seem to have any friends. She was concerned because he was so reticent in class. It was difficult to get him to speak up in oral discussions.

Background Information:

Juan and his mother, Mrs. Gallegos, came to the United States when Juan was 2 years old. Mr. Gallegos was to join the family later, but he was killed in a tragic car accident on his way to meet them. Although this accident occurred more than 8 years ago, family members say that Mrs. Gallegos has never recovered and has suffered from severe depression since that time. Juan and his mother live alone. An elderly aunt who lives down the street visits them often and helps to care for the family. Although they have many other relatives in the city, they rarely visit them because of Mrs. Gallegos's illness. She is bedridden much of the time, and she needs Juan to care for her. Juan is not allowed to go out of the yard because Mrs. Gallegos fears for his safety.

Juan started kindergarten a year late. His mother told the school she did not understand that he was to begin at the age of 5. Although his kindergarten

© 2005 by PRO-ED, Inc. All rights reserved. Duplicating this page is strictly prohibited.

CASE STUDIES

teacher wanted to have him repeat kindergarten because his socialization, language, and visual–motor skills were so poor, Juan's mother decided against this recommendation because he was already a year older than most of the other children. A year later, his first-grade teacher felt that she could not let him go on to second grade because he was doing so poorly. His second-grade teacher referred him for the special education evaluation because his work in her classroom was well below that of his peers. She decided not to recommend retention because he had been identified as having a learning disability.

 # Case Study Activity

Individual or Group Case Analysis

Answer the following questions and be prepared to discuss them in class.

1. Explain what is meant by the description, "Juan is considered to be Spanish dominant for receptive language and English dominant for expressive language." How could this influence Juan's classroom performance?

_____

_____

_____

_____

_____

_____

_____

2. What kinds of language arts activities can Juan's third-grade teacher use to assist his achievement in this area? How could assistive technology be applied to maximize instructional efforts?

_____

_____

_____

_____

_____

_____

_____

© 2005 by PRO-ED, Inc. All rights reserved. Duplicating this page is strictly prohibited.

3. What kinds of strategies can Juan's third-grade teacher use to encourage his socialization? Give four examples.

_____

_____

_____

_____

_____

_____

_____

4. What can the school do to help this family? Are there any community resources that might provide assistance to Juan and his mother?

_____

_____

_____

_____

_____

_____

_____

_____

5. When completing an assessment on a bilingual child such as Juan, how does the assessment team decide whether the educational problems are the result of the language difference or a learning disability?

_____

_____

_____

_____

_____

_____

_____

_____

© 2005 by PRO-ED, Inc. All rights reserved. Duplicating this page is strictly prohibited.

CASE STUDIES

6. Create A Question (optional)

_____

_____

_____

_____

_____

_____

_____

Kevin

Kevin is an 11-year-old fifth grader at Riverbend Elementary School. He has been receiving resource room special education services for a learning disability in the area of reading for the past 3 years. This year, the pupil assessment team has recommended that Kevin be provided special education services in the general education classroom. They have suggested that the special education teacher, Mr. Wernicke, work in collaboration with the regular education classroom teacher, Mrs. Verlo, to meet Kevin's educational needs. The team feels that Kevin should not be taken out of his fifth-grade classroom because he misses too much of the instruction that takes place in that setting and they are concerned that he will not meet the district curriculum standards.

Mrs. Verlo thinks that this change in placement is a good idea, and she is looking forward to having some extra assistance during language arts. She has just finished reading an article about the value of general and special education co-teaching in an elementary education journal, and she is eager to try this type of cooperative approach. She also believes that she will learn a good deal about special education methodology by working closely with Mr. Wernicke. Mr. Wernicke is less enthusiastic about this idea. He believes that the greatest gains in reading are made as a result of intensive remedial instruction in a one-to-one situation. He does not think that any good can come from the type of team teaching recommended by the assessment team.

Background Information:

Mr. Wernicke has been Kevin's teacher for the last 3 years. He has been using a remedial phonics approach to reading instruction. He is a very conscientious teacher who works diligently to achieve IEP goals. However, in spite of all Mr. Wernicke's efforts, Kevin has made little progress in the area of phonics. Kevin was reading a year below grade level when he was identified as having a reading disability 3 years ago. His latest composite reading scores, which were compiled for annual review, indicated that he was reading approximately $1\frac{1}{2}$ years below expectancy. While his scores for reading comprehension appear to be showing improvement, his basic reading skills (sight word vocabulary, syllabication, and phonics) are much lower.

Kevin's mother, Mrs. Mickelson, is very upset because he still is not reading on grade level. Although she likes Mr. Wernicke and feels that he is a

© 2005 by PRO-ED, Inc. All rights reserved. Duplicating this page is strictly prohibited.

dedicated teacher, she is frustrated that Kevin does not seem to be making the progress that she anticipated when she signed the placement papers for his special education services 3 years ago. Mrs. Mickelson is distressed that the gap between grade level and reading level is actually widening instead of narrowing. She supports the pupil assessment team's recommendation to keep Kevin in Mrs. Verlo's classroom for language arts, even though Mr. Wernicke has encouraged her to object to this plan.

Case Study Activity

Individual or Group Case Analysis

Answer the following questions and be prepared to discuss them in class.

1. Why has the gap between Kevin's reading level and grade level actually widened in spite of the intensive remedial reading program provided to this student? Should Mr. Wernicke be held responsible for Kevin's lack of progress?

_____

_____

_____

_____

_____

_____

_____

2. Why do you think Mr. Wernicke is so resistant to Kevin's full-time placement in the general education classroom? Give three reasons.

_____

_____

_____

_____

_____

_____

_____

© 2005 by PRO-ED, Inc. All rights reserved. Duplicating this page is strictly prohibited.

3. How could a collaborative teaching program benefit Kevin as well as the other fifth graders in Mrs. Verlo's classroom? How could assistive technology be applied to assist Kevin in meeting fifth-grade curriculum standards?

_____

_____

_____

_____

_____

_____

_____

4. What you do think about Mr. Wernicke's method of reading instruction? Has he demonstrated good decision-making skills with regard to Kevin's reading program?

_____

_____

_____

_____

_____

_____

_____

5. Next year, Kevin will make the transition from elementary school to middle school. What kind of supports will he need to be successful in this new learning environment?

_____

_____

_____

_____

_____

_____

_____

© 2005 by PRO-ED, Inc. All rights reserved. Duplicating this page is strictly prohibited.

6. Create A Question (optional)

_____

_____

_____

_____

_____

_____

_____

_____

Marta

Marta is an 18-year-old senior at Essex High School. She was diagnosed with a learning disability at the age of 7. During her school career, she was originally staffed into a self-contained classroom and then later transferred to a resource program. Marta's specific learning disability was identified in the area of reading. After 12 years of special education services, she is reading at the fourth-grade level.

Marta recently received her letter indicating that she will graduate with her class. This letter served as a "wake-up call" for her parents, Mr. and Mrs. Martinez, who promptly hired an independent evaluator to test Marta. The evaluation indicated that she was achieving at the fourth-grade level in reading and at the sixth-grade level in math. Mr. and Mrs. Martinez are furious because they feel that in spite of Marta's potential (IQ of 135), she is not prepared to do anything after graduation. They went to the principal, Mr. Vigil, with their concerns and suggested that Marta's IEP goals have not been met. Mr. Vigil dismissed their concerns by saying that Marta did not meet her goals because she was an unmotivated student. This comment made the Martinez family even angrier. They went home and started investigating private schools. They have recently written a letter to the superintendent, Mr. Greer, describing their prob-lem with the school and demanding that the district pick up the $30,000 bill for a year at a residential school that specializes in treating students who have severe learning disabilities. Mr. Greer has responded by telling Mr. Vigil to set up a meeting to resolve this problem immediately.

Background Information:

During Marta's third-grade year, the district implemented a strict, competency-based achievement program. The district put a great deal of effort into publicizing this program, and they gave district-wide parent information sessions explaining the details of this program, which was named Accountability Plus. Parents were told that these new criteria would ensure high standards for all students in the district. The district did not publicly say anything about excluding special education students from Accountability Plus, but in reality it was the district's policy not to have these students participate in the examinations for this standards program. The rationale apparently focused on the idea that special education students were inca-pable of meeting these standards, so they should be socially promoted, whereas all other students would only be promoted if standards were met.

© 2005 by PRO-ED, Inc. All rights reserved. Duplicating this page is strictly prohibited.

CASE STUDIES

Case Study Activities

Part I:
Role Playing

Break into groups of four or five students. Simulate a conference in which this problem is resolved. Assume one of the following roles: Mr. Greer, Mr. Vigil, Marta, Mr. Martinez, and Mrs. Martinez (an optional role). Provide a written summary of the resolution.

Mr. Greer, superintendent

VIEWPOINT: I don't understand these parents. Did they really want their daughter to fail every grade? Good grief! If we held this student to district standards, she would still be in the fourth grade. There's no way that we're going to pay $30,000 for this girl to go to that fancy private school. The school board will have my head if that happens!

Mr. Vigil, principal

VIEWPOINT: How did I end up with this mess? It's not my fault that this kid was socially promoted all the way through the elementary and middle school grades. What am I supposed to do, send her back to the fourth grade? Why isn't the special education director here? She should take responsibility for this mess. What are they doing in special education if they're not addressing standards? Why am I taking the heat for this debacle? I hope I don't lose my job over this. I don't want to end up back in the classroom.

Marta, student

VIEWPOINT: What am I doing here? I told my parents I didn't want to come. I can't believe that my parents are making such a big deal about this. So what if I can't read? I'm smarter than most of the kids in this school. I can get by just fine. My parents are nuts if they think I'm going to some weird school for another year after I've already graduated. Give me a break!

Mr. Martinez, Marta's father

VIEWPOINT: I'm not going to stand for this. This is outrageous! I've been paying property taxes for 25 years to support this school system and its fiascoes. Accountability Plus is a sham. These people are going to pay for this mess. What kind of a life is my child going to have with a fourth-grade reading level?

Mrs. Martinez, Marta's mother

VIEWPOINT: Marta's going to end up like me—with no choices except an early marriage. I failed all the way through school and ended up being graduated because I brown-nosed my way through enough classes to pass the requirements. It's my fault that Marta can't read—she has the very same problem that I have. She deserves better, and I'm going to get it for her. My parents couldn't do anything for me, but I'm determined to do something for her.

Resolution

_____

_____

_____

_____

_____

© 2005 by PRO-ED, Inc. All rights reserved. Duplicating this page is strictly prohibited.

_____

_____

_____

_____

_____

_____

_____

Part II:
Individual or Group Case Analysis

Answer the following questions and be prepared to discuss them in class.

1. Do you think a student who does not meet school district requirements should receive a diploma or a certificate of attendance? How should school districts resolve the issue of standards for students with disabilities?

_____

_____

_____

_____

_____

_____

2. How is it possible that Marta has a superior IQ and yet has failed to learn to read beyond an elementary school achievement level? Is Marta an example of a student who might be referred to as *twice exceptional*? Explain how this label is used by educators and why these students have needs that differ from other students with disabilities.

_____

_____

_____

_____

_____

© 2005 by PRO-ED, Inc. All rights reserved. Duplicating this page is strictly prohibited.

CASE STUDIES

3. Is Marta's school district legally responsible for the tuition for the private learning disabilities school that her parents have selected for next year? Why or why not? What laws might influence this case?

_____

_____

_____

_____

_____

_____

_____

_____

4. Could Marta go on to college when she graduates? What kinds of modifications and assistive technology could be applied to foster her success in a postsecondary environment?

_____

_____

_____

_____

_____

_____

_____

_____

5. How could the school district have handled things differently so that this problem never would have arisen? What could Mr. and Mrs. Martinez have done to prevent this situation?

_____

_____

_____

_____

_____

_____

_____

_____

© 2005 by PRO-ED, Inc. All rights reserved. Duplicating this page is strictly prohibited.

6. Create A Question (optional)

_____

_____

_____

_____

_____

_____

Susanne

Susanne is a 5-year-old child who has been identified as having a learning disability. She has been in a special education preschool classroom since the age of 3. The school district would like her to continue in this setting for another year and then go on to kindergarten in her neighborhood school. Susanne's parents, Mr. and Mrs. Devlin, are against this recommendation. They want her to be placed in her neighborhood school with her two older brothers. Mrs. Swanson, Susanne's preschool teacher, feels that the parents do not understand the ramifications of placing Susanne in a kindergarten where she will not be getting full-time special education instruction. Mr. and Mrs. Devlin are active in the Learning Disabilities Association, an organization that encourages parents to advocate for their children with learning disabilities. They have been told that the school district has an obligation to provide Susanne with the education she needs, so it is their perception that this obligation could be met in the neighborhood school just as well as it could be met in her special education setting.

Susanne's current preschool program is associated with a prestigious medical university and child development treatment center. Susanne is provided with physical therapy, occupational therapy, speech–language therapy, and intensive preacademic readiness programming on a daily basis. Her teachers and therapists are highly educated and trained. Mr. and Mrs. Devlin have not been dissatisfied with Susanne's program there, but they have become increasingly uncomfortable with the fact that their daughter's preschool is in a medical school as opposed to being in a neighborhood setting. As they have become more involved with the Learning Disabilities Association, they have listened to parents speak about the pros and cons of segregated settings for their children. They have gradually come to the conclusion that Susanne's social needs should be a priority for her kindergarten year.

The staff at Susanne's school has suggested that it would be a big mistake for Susanne to go to the neighborhood school. They believe that her functioning is so low that she would not be able to participate in the kindergarten curriculum, which has expectations for students to begin reading by the end of the school year. They also feel that the public school's emphasis on the standards-based curriculum and state assessments will not allow for the individual attention that Susanne needs in a kindergarten classroom. Mrs. Swanson is very much attached to Susanne. She has worked laboriously with this child to get her to the level at which she is currently functioning. She and her colleagues feel that Susanne will lose all of these hard-won skills if they are not reinforced. Mrs.

© 2005 by PRO-ED, Inc. All rights reserved. Duplicating this page is strictly prohibited.

CASE STUDIES

Swanson feels that if she had one more year to work with Susanne, she could provide an intensive focus on readiness skills that would give her the firm foundation to experience more success in the elementary school years. It is very distressing for her to think that the Devlins could give up Susanne's highly specialized program at the medical school for a public school program.

Background Information:

From an early age, Mrs. Devlin knew that Susanne was not demonstrating normal achievement of developmental milestones. Susanne did not walk or talk until she was almost 2 years of age. When she did begin walking, she seemed to have to concentrate on each step as she moved from point to point. While Susanne's siblings had started showing an interest in coloring at the age of 2, Susanne still couldn't hold a crayon or marker until close to age 4. She seemed to have a very difficult time expressing herself. Often she appeared to know what she wanted to say, but the words did not come out. Instead of using words, she would use sounds to tell family members that she had seen an airplane or a fire truck. Susanne's pediatrician agreed with Mrs. Devlin that Susanne should be pro-

vided with a complete developmental evaluation. He referred the family to the medical school.

Susanne's evaluation revealed significant language and visual–motor problems. Although Susanne's receptive language was found to be within the range of normal functioning, her expressive language was 2 years below expectancy. The speech therapist who completed the evaluation told Mr. and Mrs. Devlin that Susanne's language skills were so low that her performance was comparable to that of a child who had been deprived of normal language stimulation, "as if she had been locked in a closet for most of her life." Susanne's motor milestones were so far below expectation that the psychologist diagnosed her as having "subclinical cerebral palsy," meaning that her motor problems were almost severe enough to meet the criteria for cerebral palsy. Her final diagnosis was that of severe learning disability. The Devlins were devastated when the evaluation team gave the results to them. The team made it clear to the family that Susanne would always have "an uphill battle trying to be like other children." But they also assured the Devlins that through an intensive school program like the one at the medical university, Susanne would be able to make substantial progress. The Devlins signed her up for the program during that same meeting.

Case Study Activities

Part I:
Individual Learning Plan

Assume the role of a kindergarten teacher and write a two-page narrative explaining how you could meet Susanne's needs in your standards-based classroom. Included in this narrative should be a description of (a) accommodations for language, visual–motor, and social needs; (b) examples of specific strategies for readiness skills; (c) an evaluation system to determine progress; (d) resources, including assistive technology, to be used; and (e) transition supports.

Part II:
Individual or Group Case Analysis

In the space on the next page, provide at least five reasons why Susanne should go to her neighborhood school for kindergarten and another five reasons why she should go back to the special education program at the medical university. Then decide which appears to be the preferable setting and write a paragraph explaining why that particular recommendation seems to be the most appropriate for this child.

© 2005 by PRO-ED, Inc. All rights reserved. Duplicating this page is strictly prohibited.

Neighborhood School   Special Education School

_____   _____

_____   _____

_____   _____

_____   _____

_____   _____

Recommendation

_____

_____

_____

_____

_____

_____

_____

_____

_____

_____

_____

_____

_____

_____

_____

_____

_____

_____

© 2005 by PRO-ED, Inc. All rights reserved. Duplicating this page is strictly prohibited.

CASE STUDIES

CHAPTER 2

Mental Retardation

Eli

Eli is a 7-year-old first grader at Green Acres Elementary School. He has Down syndrome. Eli is a quiet, compliant little boy with a pleasant disposition. He is often described as an inactive child. His activity level is so low that he often appears to be lethargic. Eli also has hypotonia, which causes him to be somewhat awkward in fine and gross motor activities. Mrs. Gianetti, his first-grade teacher, is a very warm, loving individual who has welcomed Eli into her class. Of the four first-grade teachers in the building, Mrs. Gianetti was the only teacher who expressed a willingness to have Eli in her classroom. Her attitude is that everyone should be included in the mainstream of life, even though her expectations for Eli are clearly different from those she holds for her other first graders.

Mrs. Gianetti has designed a "cozy corner" exclusively for Eli. In this area, she has placed overstuffed pillows, a quilt, and a variety of preschool picture books. She encourages Eli to spend as much time as he likes in this corner. It is not unusual for him to fall asleep there in the early afternoon and spend 2 hours napping. Mrs. Gianetti spends her own money to buy coloring books for Eli to use in the classroom, which he thoroughly enjoys. She also brings toys (discards from her grandchildren) to school for him to play with. Eli adores Mrs. Gianetti and the affection is returned. Mrs. Gianetti is proud of her inclusion efforts and considers herself to be somewhat of a disability activist because of her acceptance of this child in her classroom.

Background Information:

Eli's parents, Mr. and Mrs. Hamberg, do not want Eli to be in a special education program. They believe that he will do his best if he is challenged in the general education curriculum. Last year, when the pupil assessment team recommended that Eli be provided with $2\frac{1}{2}$ hours of resource help on a daily basis, they adamantly refused to consider the suggestion or to sign the papers for special education placement. They were delighted when they were informed that there was a first-grade teacher who was willing to have Eli in her classroom. They could not have been more pleased when they met Mrs. Gianetti and observed her to be such an accepting and caring individual.

For the first month of the school year, the Hambergs were pleased with Eli's enthusiasm for school, which confirmed their notions regarding the appropriateness of the setting for his needs. They began having second thoughts when Mrs. Hamberg dropped in unexpectedly to bring a rain parka for Eli. Mrs. Hamberg was taken aback when she found Eli in the corner sleeping, while the rest of the class was having math. After that experience, the Hambergs began dropping in frequently. Almost every time they visited, they observed Eli engaged in coloring, playing with toys, or sleeping in his corner. Last week things came to a head when Mrs. Hamberg found Eli sleeping in the corner for the third afternoon in a row. She waited until school was dismissed and then very calmly and firmly explained to Mrs. Gianetti that Eli's curriculum was "totally inappropriate" and would no longer be acceptable. Mrs. Hamberg further stated that from this point forward, she wanted Eli to do whatever the other first graders were doing, and she wanted his "cozy corner" dismantled.

The conference was abruptly terminated when Mrs. Gianetti burst into tears and left for the principal's office. Through a rush of tears, Mrs. Gianetti told the principal that after all she had done for Eli and his family, none of her efforts were appreciated and, in fact, she was being harshly criticized for her hard work. That same afternoon the principal called an emergency meeting of all the first-grade teachers and asked them to reconsider having Eli placed in one of their classes because the placement with Mrs. Gianetti was not working out. They were vociferous in their defense of Mrs. Gianetti and made remarks to the effect that the parents should be grateful that Mrs. Gianetti even accepted "a child like that" in her class. They were also steadfastly unanimous in their refusal to have Eli moved to one of their classrooms.

© 2005 by PRO-ED, Inc. All rights reserved. Duplicating this page is strictly prohibited.

CASE STUDIES

Case Study Activity

Individual or Group Case Analysis

Answer the following questions and be prepared to discuss them in class.

1. Was Eli provided access to the general education curriculum in Mrs. Gianetti's classroom? How could this teacher have more successfully integrated Eli into a standards-based first-grade curriculum?

_____

_____

_____

_____

_____

_____

2. What assistive technology supports could have increased the effectiveness of instruction for Eli?

_____

_____

_____

_____

_____

_____

3. Do the other three first-grade teachers have a right to reject Eli as one of their students? Why or why not? If you were the principal, what would you do in this situation?

_____

_____

_____

_____

_____

_____

© 2005 by PRO-ED, Inc. All rights reserved. Duplicating this page is strictly prohibited.

4. Are Eli's parents unrealistic about his potential? Because they rejected the special education services, do they have a right to criticize Mrs. Gianetti's approach to instruction?

_____

_____

_____

_____

_____

_____

_____

5. Could Mr. and Mrs. Hamberg have handled this situation in a way that might have caused fewer hurtful and angry feelings? What might they have done differently?

_____

_____

_____

_____

_____

_____

_____

6. Create A Question (optional)

_____

_____

_____

_____

_____

_____

_____

© 2005 by PRO-ED, Inc. All rights reserved. Duplicating this page is strictly prohibited.

CASE STUDIES

Elizabeth

Elizabeth is a 10-year-old child in the third grade at Bennett Elementary School. She has multiple disabilities including cerebral palsy, severe mental retardation, moderate hearing loss, and a seizure disorder. This is Elizabeth's second year in general education. Last year did not go very well for Elizabeth. Her second-grade teacher showed little interest in including her in academic activities, so for the most part Elizabeth sat in her chair, waiting for her special education teacher, occupational therapist, or speech therapist to come and get her. The special education staff had wanted to provide therapy for Elizabeth in the second-grade classroom, but the teacher declined, saying that it was too distracting for the other students. Elizabeth's teacher this year, Mrs. Gables, is determined that Elizabeth is going to be an active member of the class. She has not had any experience with children like Elizabeth, so she has asked Mrs. Jennings, the special education teacher, to help her.

Elizabeth relies on the use of a wheelchair because she has paraplegia as a result of the cerebral palsy. Although she can use her arms, her movements are characterized by spasticity. Mrs. Gables feels that Elizabeth should be using a desk like the other children in the classroom, but she does not know if she should be moving her in and out of the wheelchair. When Mrs. Gables brought this up to Elizabeth's mother, Mrs. Valle, she was told that Elizabeth would be fine in her chair. Her mother said that Mrs. Gables did not need to be straining her back by moving Elizabeth in and out of her desk because it did not matter to Elizabeth where she sat.

Mrs. Gables has also mentioned to Mrs. Valle that Elizabeth asks for food during lunch, and she wonders if she is getting enough to eat. Elizabeth is tube fed by the school nurse prior to going to the cafeteria. It bothers Mrs. Gables that Elizabeth just sits there looking hungry while the other children are eating. Again, Mrs. Valle told her not to worry. She said that her tube feeding provided her with all the nourishment she needed. She also said that Elizabeth would have food all over herself, and the other kids would have a field day teasing her if she started eating in the cafeteria. Mrs. Gables has the impression that Mrs. Valle is not interested in having Elizabeth

participate during lunch. Sometimes she feels that Elizabeth's mother does not care about Elizabeth's curriculum at school. She does not like to be critical of parents, but she cannot help feeling that something is not right with this parent–child relationship.

Mrs. Gables is planning a unit on transportation, and she would like Elizabeth to be able to participate. She has asked Mrs. Jennings to come into her room and work with her on this unit, so that she can better understand what adaptations and modifications Elizabeth needs. Mrs. Jennings said that she would be delighted to work with Mrs. Gables on "curriculum overlapping" for the transportation unit. Mrs. Jennings explained to Mrs. Gables that this is a technique whereby the content is examined to determine how it can be modified for students who are working on other objectives. Mrs. Jennings is currently working with Elizabeth on number concepts, range of motion, and vocabulary. She mentioned to Mrs. Gables that this transportation unit would be an ideal place to start because the content would probably be motivating to Elizabeth, as her father is an airline pilot. Mrs. Gables is glad that Mrs. Jennings will be working closely with her because she has no idea where to start teaching Elizabeth.

Background Information:

Elizabeth was adopted when she was 2 days old by Mr. and Mrs. Valle, who had tried for years to have children of their own. During the first 6 months of life, it became obvious to the Valles that Elizabeth was not developing as expected. However, they did not find out the full extent of her disabilities until she was almost 2 years old. Mrs. Valle became deeply depressed when she came to the realization that Elizabeth would never walk and would be severely mentally retarded with limited communication skills. At that time, she told her husband that she wanted to give Elizabeth back to the adoption agency, but he would not hear of it. Mr. Valle wanted to adopt another child; however, Mrs. Valle would not agree unless Elizabeth was relinquished. This disagreement became a major point of contention that was never resolved.

After Elizabeth was diagnosed as having multiple disabilities, Mrs. Valle hired a full-time, live-in

© 2005 by PRO-ED, Inc. All rights reserved. Duplicating this page is strictly prohibited.

nanny to care for Elizabeth because she did not feel that she was able to do this. Mr. Valle became immersed in his work and signed on for more international flights, which resulted in spending less and less time at home. Mrs. Valle began spending less time with her daughter and started taking up a variety of hobbies and volunteer work that kept her very busy. Last year, Mrs. Valle had an apartment added on to their house. She moved the nanny and Elizabeth into this addition. Since the parents have not told the nanny what kinds of activities they would like her to involve Elizabeth in, the two of them spend most of their time in front of the television.

Although Elizabeth has the physical abilities to mouth feed, her mother told the nanny that she finds it more convenient and less messy to use the tube feeding procedure. The occupational therapist at Bennett Elementary School has offered to start feeding Elizabeth food during lunch so she can feel like she is participating more, but Mrs. Valle did not seem too happy with this idea. She told the therapist that she doubted very much if Elizabeth cared one way or the other. The therapist decided not to pursue it at the time because of Mrs. Valle's attitude, but she is definitely going to bring it up again at the annual review.

Case Study Activity

Individual or Group Case Analysis

Answer the following questions and be prepared to discuss them in class.

1. Is there any way the school can work with this family to get the parents more involved in this child's life? Describe three strategies you might use if you were Mrs. Gables.

_____

_____

_____

_____

_____

_____

_____

_____

_____

© 2005 by PRO-ED, Inc. All rights reserved. Duplicating this page is strictly prohibited.

CASE STUDIES

2. Do you think Elizabeth should be eating food in the cafeteria with the other students at lunchtime? Why might this be important for Elizabeth? Do you think Mrs. Valle's concerns about teasing are valid?

_____

_____

_____

_____

_____

_____

3. Do you think the goal of transference from the wheelchair to the desk might be an appropriate one for this child? Why would it be important for a child who uses a wheelchair to be taken out of the chair and placed in a variety of different positions?

_____

_____

_____

_____

_____

_____

4. Explain how Mrs. Jennings and Mrs. Gables could teach number concepts and vocabulary, as well as increase range of motion during the upcoming transportation unit. Describe a sample transportation lesson from this unit, and explain how it can be modified to address these three skills for Elizabeth.

_____

_____

_____

_____

_____

_____

© 2005 by PRO-ED, Inc. All rights reserved. Duplicating this page is strictly prohibited.

5. What kinds of assistive technology could be used to maximize success for Elizabeth in the areas of communication and reading?

_____

_____

_____

_____

_____

6. Create A Question (optional)

_____

_____

_____

_____

_____

Hwa-Fang

Hwa-Fang is a 9-year-old student at Canalside Elementary. She has recently begun first grade in Mrs. London's class. Mrs. London has been told that Hwa-Fang probably has mental retardation and that she has an expressive vocabulary of approximately only 10 words. She also has mild spastic cerebral palsy and seizures that are mostly controlled with the help of anti-epileptic drugs. Hwa-Fang was evaluated last year in kindergarten. The results of this evaluation revealed that her IQ was 60. Adaptive skills, as measured by the _Vineland Adaptive Behavior Scales_ (Sparrow, Balla, & Cicchetti, 1984), were found to be significantly below age level. It was recommended that Hwa-Fang be placed in a full-time special education class, which would concentrate on teaching her English and remediating the areas of weakness that had

been identified by this evaluation. Mr. and Mrs. Epstein, Hwa-Fang's parents, disagreed with the evaluation and refused the special education placement. They want her in the general education classroom and are willing to hire professionals on a private basis to provide her with speech–language therapy, occupational–physical therapy, and academic remediation outside of school.

Background Information:

Hwa-Fang was born in a remote, rural area of China. Her biological parents abandoned her on the steps of an American missionary's home. Hwa-Fang was taken to an orphanage in Beijing and lived there for 8 years. She was not adopted because of her cerebral palsy. At the age of 8, the missionary family who originally

© 2005 by PRO-ED, Inc. All rights reserved. Duplicating this page is strictly prohibited.

CASE STUDIES

cared for her arranged for an adoption of Hwa-Fang by a family in the United States.

Hwa-Fang's adoptive parents are both attorneys in their late forties. They have no other children. Mr. and Mrs. Epstein are active in their community. Mrs. Epstein is employed by the American Civil Liberties Union and contributes a great deal of volunteer time to Amnesty International. Mr. Epstein works for the state immigration and naturalization agency and contributes many hours of community service to the Jewish Anti-Defamation League. The Epsteins are committed to giving this child the best opportunities this country has to offer.

Given that Hwa-Fang was small for her age, developmentally delayed, and could not speak English, the principal placed her in kindergarten even though she was 8 years old when she entered Canalside. The principal also recommended a complete special education evaluation for Hwa-Fang. Mr. and Mrs. Epstein welcomed the recommended evaluation. They looked forward to the staffing where they were to hear the re-

sults of Hwa-Fang's testing. However, they were bitterly disappointed with the results. Their main contention was that Hwa-Fang does not know enough English to have her intelligence tested. It made no difference to them when they were told that a nonverbal intelligence test was used with Hwa-Fang. They were incredulous that a child with cerebral palsy was tested by a measure largely dependent upon visual–motor proficiency. Mr. and Mrs. Epstein were outraged that professionals would use such inappropriate measurement techniques to come up with what they considered to be a prejudiced diagnosis of mental retardation. They see this assessment as an attempt to pigeonhole their child into a low-achieving track where she will not receive the necessary stimulation to spur achievement. In no uncertain terms, they let the school know that they would not allow Hwa-Fang to receive any special services during the school day, and any further attempt to label her as mentally retarded would result in litigation.

Case Study Activity

Individual or Group Case Analysis

Answer the following questions and be prepared to discuss them in class.

1. Would it be considered good practice for the school system to assess Hwa-Fang's intelligence with standardized tests? What other testing alternatives would be available for use with a child like Hwa-Fang?

_____

_____

_____

_____

_____

_____

_____

© 2005 by PRO-ED, Inc. All rights reserved. Duplicating this page is strictly prohibited.

2. Do you support the parents' position to withhold special education services during the school day? Why or why not?

_____

_____

_____

_____

_____

_____

_____

3. If you were Hwa-Fang's teacher, how would you attempt to increase her English skills within your language arts program? Give at least three examples of assistive technology that could be used to promote her skills in this area.

_____

_____

_____

_____

_____

_____

_____

_____

4. If you were Hwa-Fang's teacher, how would you work with her family to increase the effectiveness of your classroom instruction?

_____

_____

_____

_____

_____

_____

_____

© 2005 by PRO-ED, Inc. All rights reserved. Duplicating this page is strictly prohibited.

CASE STUDIES

5. Do you think Hwa-Fang's diagnosis of mental retardation is biased? Is there any other explanation for her low performance on the test of adaptive behavior? Is an IQ test that focuses on visual–motor performance an appropriate choice for this child?

_____

_____

_____

_____

_____

_____

6. Create A Question (optional)

_____

_____

_____

_____

_____

_____

Lemar

Lemar is a 6-year-old kindergarten student at Pine Knolls Elementary. He was diagnosed with Fragile X syndrome at the age of 2. He has spent the last 3 years in a special education preschool setting. This will be his first year in a general education classroom. Lemar has the prominent physical characteristics associated with Fragile X, such as large ears, a broad forehead, and a long narrow face. His most recent evaluation indicates mild mental retardation with both language and visual–motor skill development in the 3- to 4-year range. Lemar's behavioral characteristics include short attention span and autistic-like actions such as hand flapping, toe walking, and poor eye contact. In addition to these difficulties, Lemar is hypersensitive to touch, smell, taste, and hearing. He also engages in self-injurious behavior, particularly hand biting. It is not unusual for him to draw blood if he is not carefully monitored. Although Mrs. Reid, his kindergarten teacher, is not exactly thrilled with the prospect of having Lemar in her class, she is a committed

© 2005 by PRO-ED, Inc. All rights reserved. Duplicating this page is strictly prohibited.

teacher who takes her responsibilities seriously. The principal has arranged to have a paraprofessional with Lemar for 1 hour of the 2½-hour kindergarten day.

Background Information:

Lemar has an 11-year-old brother, Andre, who also has Fragile X syndrome. Andre was institutionalized last year because of behavioral problems including vandalism, stealing, and truancy. Andre's difficulties escalated at the age of 7. When he was being evaluated at that time, the school psychologist noted that baby Lemar shared the same physical features associated with Fragile X. He recommended that their mother, Mrs. Prutch, have Lemar tested. Lemar was evaluated through Child Find and diagnosed with the same genetic disorder. The major difference between the brothers is that Andre has learning disabilities, whereas Lemar has mental retardation. Andre is also hypersensitive, and it is this sensitivity to stimulation that results in his violent outbursts of temper. Andre's behavioral incidents are usually triggered by touching, pushing, or teasing.

Mrs. Prutch is a single parent with limited resources. She supports her family through welfare, as the father abandoned the family shortly after Lemar's birth. Although Mrs. Prutch apparently provides for Lemar's physical needs, she appears to have limited energy for other parenting responsibilities.

Lemar's preschool years were somewhat problematic because of his behavior. His hypersensitivity caused him to respond adversely to smells from the cafeteria, normal sounds from the building, and any type of visual distraction. For example, if certain strong odors, such as those from pizza or tacos, drifted up to the classroom, Lemar would react by holding his nose, screaming, and rolling around on the floor. Similar behaviors were demonstrated when the public address system was used or when the bell rang. In addition to these behaviors, his self-abusive hand biting was a constant source of concern for his teachers. Whenever they tried to enlist the help of Mrs. Prutch in a behavior management program, she would fail to show up for meetings or return their phone calls. In the special education setting of 11 students, a teacher, and an aide, it was all the staff could do to keep Lemar from seriously injuring himself. His special education teacher recommended that he be placed in a self-contained special needs kindergarten. The school district did not follow this recommendation, as they have recently adopted a policy of inclusion for all students with disabilities who have the potential to benefit from the general education environment.

Case Study Activity

Individual or Group Case Analysis

Answer the following questions and be prepared to discuss them in class.

1. What can Mrs. Reid do in her classroom to help Lemar with his hypersensitivity and hand biting? Give three specific suggestions for each.

_____

_____

_____

_____

_____

© 2005 by PRO-ED, Inc. All rights reserved. Duplicating this page is strictly prohibited.

2. What transition supports would enhance Lemar's successful integration into a general education kindergarten classroom?

_____

_____

_____

_____

_____

_____

_____

3. If you were Mrs. Reid, how would you provide Lemar with access to the standards-based kindergarten curriculum in the area of language arts? How could assistive technology provide support to this child?

_____

_____

_____

_____

_____

_____

_____

4. Do you think Lemar will eventually be placed in a residential facility like his brother, Andre? How could his chances for successful school and community integration be increased?

_____

_____

_____

_____

_____

_____

_____

© 2005 by PRO-ED, Inc. All rights reserved. Duplicating this page is strictly prohibited.

5. List four possible reasons why Mrs. Prutch has not been involved in Lemar's educational planning thus far. If you were Mrs. Reid, how would you attempt to establish and sustain communication with this parent?

_____

_____

_____

_____

_____

_____

6. Create A Question (optional)

_____

_____

_____

_____

_____

_____

Sammy

Sammy is an 8-year-old first-grade student at River Ridge Elementary. His teacher, Mrs. Lopez, is having a very difficult time integrating this child into her class of 25 students. He has been diagnosed as mildly mentally retarded with accompanying attention-deficit/hyperactivity disorder. He receives special education support services for 1 hour each morning and spends the remaining time in the first-grade classroom. Academically, he is working on a readiness level in reading and math. His fine motor skills are quite poor, and he cannot write his name or numbers legibly. Although these academic difficulties are of concern to Mrs. Lopez, it is Sammy's behavior that is more pressing at this point. This child is extremely impulsive. He cannot seem to stay seated for more than 2 or 3 minutes without supervision. He is also very aggressive and frequently hits, pushes, and kicks the other children with only the slightest provocation. He has no friends and does not seem to understand how to play or work with others. In spite of these problems, Sammy demonstrates a real interest in learning when he is able to attend to instructional material. It is not unusual for him to bring a book over to Mrs. Lopez and ask her to help him read or to tell her that he has

© 2005 by PRO-ED, Inc. All rights reserved. Duplicating this page is strictly prohibited.

CASE STUDIES

learned a new word. Mrs. Lopez feels that he has untapped potential, but she is concerned that it will take years to make significant progress unless his behavior can be managed more effectively.

Background Information:

Sammy was held back in kindergarten because of concerns regarding his development. He was referred for special education evaluation at the beginning of this year. In addition to his mental retardation, attentional deficits, and hyperactivity, he displays characteristics that indicate he may have fetal alcohol syndrome. This could not be confirmed because Sammy's father, Mr. Ferrer, would not take him for the pediatric evaluation.

Mrs. Lopez has also tried to get Mr. Ferrer involved with Sammy's school problems, but she has had little cooperation. Sammy's previous teachers have expressed concern and frustration about this child's family situation. He lives with his father, who will not supply any information about Sammy's mother. She apparently left the family shortly after Sammy was born and has no contact with him. Sammy is consistently dirty and often wears ripped clothing (his peers report that he usually does not wear underwear). He has no siblings, and teachers have the impression that he is often left alone by his father. When Mr. Ferrer has been asked to come to school for conferences, he almost always declines, saying that he cannot miss work. The one time he did come to school was when he signed the papers for Sammy's special education placement. On that occasion, when asked if he would be willing to participate in a behavior management program that involved a home–school behavior notebook, he declined saying, "I don't want you to go to any extra trouble for him, he just ain't worth it." When the school personnel protested the remark, Mr. Ferrer quickly left.

Case Study Activity

Individual or Group Case Analysis

Answer the following questions and be prepared to discuss them in class.

1. How could Mrs. Lopez motivate Mr. Ferrer to come to school to discuss Sammy's progress? Do you think that a teacher can make a difference for a child such as this?

_____

_____

_____

_____

_____

_____

_____

_____

© 2005 by PRO-ED, Inc. All rights reserved. Duplicating this page is strictly prohibited.

2. Does Sammy's current living situation constitute abuse or neglect? What can Mrs. Lopez do about Sammy's home life?

_____

_____

_____

_____

_____

_____

_____

3. What are some of the characteristics of fetal alcohol syndrome (FAS)? From an instructional perspective, does a diagnosis of FAS provide implications for teaching?

_____

_____

_____

_____

_____

_____

_____

4. What kinds of strategies could Mrs. Lopez use to decrease Sammy's impulsivity and aggressive behavior?

_____

_____

_____

_____

_____

_____

_____

© 2005 by PRO-ED, Inc. All rights reserved. Duplicating this page is strictly prohibited.

CASE STUDIES

5. What types of assistive technology might be helpful for fostering development of Sammy's readiness skills?

_____

_____

_____

_____

_____

_____

6. Create A Question (optional)

_____

_____

_____

_____

_____

_____

Vincent

Vincent is an 18-year-old senior at Lincoln High School. He was diagnosed with mild mental retardation when he was in the first grade. Since this time, he has been in self-contained special education classrooms for all instruction except for physical education, music, and art. In a couple of months, he will graduate and begin a job with a local pizza restaurant chain. He has received job preparation training through a life skills program at Lincoln.

For the past year, Vincent has been complaining to his parents, Mr. and Mrs. Mancuso, that he does not want to go to work for Pizza Prince when he finishes school. He says he is sick of pizza and wants to get a job working on the assembly line of a local auto manufacturer. Mrs. Mancuso has spoken to Mr. Keating, Vincent's special education teacher, who says it simply would not be possible for Vincent to hold that type of employment. Although Mr. Keating did not come right out and say it, Mrs. Mancuso got the definite impression that he felt Vincent was lucky that Pizza Prince had offered him a job at competitive pay—that is, minimum wage. Most of Mr. Keating's students in the life skills program are paid much less than that.

When Mrs. Mancuso told Vincent that he had no other choice but to take this job, Vincent got very

© 2005 by PRO-ED, Inc. All rights reserved. Duplicating this page is strictly prohibited.

angry and told his parents he was going to drop out of school and spend the next few months looking for another kind of job. This distressed both Mr. and Mrs. Mancuso. They are looking forward to Vincent graduating with a high school diploma, an accomplishment that neither of them were able to attain.

Background Information:

When Vincent was originally diagnosed with mental retardation, his IQ was determined to be 62 on the full scale of the *Wechsler Intelligence Scale for Children–Third Edition* (WISC—III; Wechsler, 1991), with a performance scale of 67 and a verbal scale of 57. Vincent had a very difficult time with language processing and was originally referred for evaluation because of suspected problems in this area. It was determined that Vincent would probably have a better opportunity for learning in a self-contained classroom where the teacher could help him with his language difficulties on a one-to-one or small-group basis. Vincent enjoyed his elementary and middle school years. He spoke positively of his special education teachers and appeared to like socializing with his classmates. He did not see his classmates over the weekends because they lived in different neighborhoods, so he was always eager to return to school on Monday morning.

His high school years did not go as well for Vincent. The friends he had made in elementary and middle school went to a different high school. The students that were in his life skills classroom were, for the most part, lower functioning than Vincent. He soon found that he had nothing in common with most of them. Mr. and Mrs. Mancuso were surprised and upset when they discovered that Vincent was no longer in a classroom with students who were similar to him, but Mr. Keating explained that Vincent could be given a more appropriate education for his needs along with the individualized attention for his language problems in a classroom such as this. Out of the eight students in this classroom, three were autistic, two had severe retardation, and two had moderate retardation. Vincent was the only student who was functioning in the mild range of mental retardation. Mr. Keating told the Mancusos that if Vincent stayed in this program, he could assure them that he would receive a high school diploma, but if he were in the mainstream he was not sure that would happen. Mr. Keating felt that the demands of the general educa-

tion classroom would be such that Vincent would become discouraged and drop out. He also told them that if Vincent stayed in his program, he could almost guarantee them that Vincent would be gainfully employed by the time he left high school. Even though Mr. and Mrs. Mancuso continued to worry about Vincent's unhappiness, they felt he must stay in Mr. Keating's program for his own benefit.

The major objective of the life skills program at Lincoln is to find an appropriate vocational area for each student and to assist with the development of transition skills to help the student move from school to community life. Mr. Keating's program provided the students with two employment options—food service and janitorial. Two major companies contracted with Lincoln so that life skills class graduates would be guaranteed jobs when they left school. Mr. Keating conducts an extensive potential profile of each of his students before they are placed in either janitorial or food service. However, that was not the case with Vincent, as he informed Mr. Keating on the first day of class that, "I ain't going to be no janitor." Mr. Keating felt that all students deserved flexibility whenever it could be provided, so he placed Vincent in the food service program with the students who had autism or severe mental retardation.

Although Vincent never liked the Pizza Prince program, he did not talk much about it. In fact, during his high school years, he became distant and did not interact with his parents or friends as he had in years before. Mr. and Mrs. Mancuso felt that he was just going through a stage, so they did not worry too much. They were grateful that he did not get into trouble like many of their friends' teenagers. But now that he has talked about dropping out, they are very upset. They are frustrated by Mr. Keating, but they are afraid to say anything more to him. They cannot understand why working at a pizza restaurant is the only job that their son can hold.

Mr. Keating is feeling frustrated about Vincent and his family as well. He has spent a great deal of time with this student, and he feels very proud that Vincent will be employed on a competitive basis. He is also very proud of his life skills class, which is considered to be a model program in the city. It bothers him that instead of thanking him, the Mancusos seem to be indirectly criticizing him. He really does not understand what they expect.

© 2005 by PRO-ED, Inc. All rights reserved. Duplicating this page is strictly prohibited.

CASE STUDIES

Case Study Activity

Individual or Group Case Analysis

Answer the following questions and be prepared to discuss them in class.

1. Do you think Vincent is at risk for dropping out of school? Why or why not?

_____

_____

_____

_____

_____

_____

2. Explain Mr. Keating's position on vocational training for students with disabilities. Should a student like Vincent have other options in addition to janitorial and food service? Is the school district responsible for developing vocational programs that meet the needs of all students with disabilities?

_____

_____

_____

_____

_____

_____

3. In addition to disliking food service, is there another reason why Vincent does not like this vocational program? What modifications could be made to alleviate this problem?

_____

_____

_____

_____

_____

_____

© 2005 by PRO-ED, Inc. All rights reserved. Duplicating this page is strictly prohibited.

4. What is the possibility that an individual like Vincent could be trained for a job in auto manufacturing? Is competitive compensation the most important criteria for job training? Would it make sense for an individual to earn less in a job that he preferred? Explain your answer.

_____

_____

_____

_____

_____

_____

_____

5. How could the school work with this student and his family to resolve this problem?

_____

_____

_____

_____

_____

_____

_____

6. Create A Question (optional)

_____

_____

_____

_____

_____

_____

_____

© 2005 by PRO-ED, Inc. All rights reserved. Duplicating this page is strictly prohibited.

CASE STUDIES

CHAPTER 3

Attention Deficit with Hyperactivity Disorder

Casey

Casey is an 8-year-old second grader at East Valley Elementary. His teacher, Mrs. Bromwell, is having a difficult time with his behavior. Casey has an excessive activity level that makes it difficult for him to attend to one task for longer than 5 minutes. He seems to have so much energy that he cannot stand still. Casey will sometimes get up from his desk and start jumping up and down at what seems to be a frenetic pace. This is a typical behavior that causes classroom problems. He does not stop until Mrs. Bromwell comes over and gently assists him in finding his chair. He has literally worn a hole in the carpet next to his desk. Sometimes he will hop around the room, running into other children's desks, knocking over bookcases, and accidentally pushing other children around. He talks "a mile a minute," but he rarely says anything that is of interest to the other children. Casey is in perpetual motion, as if he is being driven to the point of frenzy. Needless to say, this kind of behavior gets on everyone's nerves. He is very unpopular with the other children because he is always accidentally tripping over someone or ruining someone's art project by spilling paint or glue. He even gets in trouble during recess, either because he is moving too fast to listen to the instructions of the game, or because he will not let another student have a turn when he is fixated on a particular activity. For example, he refuses to relinquish the bat until he gets a base hit. Mrs. Bromwell has had many active kindergarteners in her 15 years of teaching, but she has never seen a child like Casey.

Casey's behavior is Mrs. Bromwell's main concern because she feels that it interferes with the achievement of the entire class. Since Casey cannot stay focused on his work, he inadvertently bothers the students who are trying to stay on task. Mrs. Bromwell is also concerned about Casey's academic achievement. His handwriting is completely illegible, and she believes his reading and math skills are well below grade level; however, she's not certain that she has been able to obtain an accurate estimation of his abilities because of his attentional difficulties. She initiated a special education evaluation, but was told by the prereferral team coordinator that Casey would not qualify because his standardized test scores revealed he was functioning within the average range

for his grade placement. Mrs. Bromwell could hardly believe this so she looked up the scores in his cumulative folder and was surprised to find verification of grade level functioning.

Background Information:

Casey was originally referred for special education evaluation in kindergarten. His kindergarten teacher had informed the parents that she had never seen a child as hyperactive as Casey and that he would not learn anything unless he was put on medication. This teacher felt that his problems were so significant that having him repeat kindergarten would do little for him unless he was supported with medication. Mr. and Mrs. Donovan, Casey's parents, were surprised that the teacher recommended medicating a five-year-old, but they immediately took him to their pediatrician who referred Casey to a neurologist at the Children's Hospital. The neurologist and a team of specialists determined that Casey was neurologically impaired and diagnosed attention-deficit disorder with hyperactivity. Medication was prescribed to treat the activity level and attentional problems. As soon as he began the medication, his school work and behavior improved dramatically. Consequently, the parents did not see the need to follow up with the special education evaluation procedures at school. With the help of his medication, Casey had a very successful year in first grade. His handwriting became legible and his standardized achievement scores ranged from the 50th to 60th percentile for first grade. However, over the summer following first grade, Casey began having significant side effects from the medication, including insomia and facial tics. His insomnia was so bad that he was sleeping less than 4 hours per night. Casey developed "amphetamine eyes," the dark circles characteristic of an individual who is abusing amphetamines. His neurologist tried many other psychostimulant medications, but the insomnia did not abate and the facial tics worsened. When nonpsychostimulant medications were tried, they were ineffective for controlling the hyperactivity and distractibility. Mr. and Mrs. Donovan decided that Casey would have no more medication regardless of the educational consequences. The parents are very upset because the facial tics have continued even after the

© 2005 by PRO-ED, Inc. All rights reserved. Duplicating this page is strictly prohibited.

CASE STUDIES

medication was stopped. Although the neurologist believes that they will eventually stop, he cannot predict when this will happen. So now Casey has one more obvious problem added to his other difficulties.

The parents are of the opinion that the school is not doing all that it should to assist Casey in achieving educational goals. They have suggested that if the school had done a better job with him in kindergarten, he would never have been on the medication and would not be in the predicament he is in now. It was not surprising that when Casey returned to school in second grade, he demonstrated the same behaviors that his kindergarten teacher had observed.

Case Study Activity

Individual or Group Analysis

Answer the following questions and be prepared to discuss them in class.

1. Could Casey qualify for special education support in spite of what the referral team coordinator told Mrs. Bromwell? What laws might influence this case?

_____

_____

_____

_____

_____

_____

_____

2. Is it realistic to think that Mrs. Bromwell could meet the needs of both Casey and the other students in her class without outside support? What kind of a behavior management plan might be effective for this student? Give an example of such a plan and identify specific supports and strategies that would be included.

_____

_____

_____

_____

_____

_____

_____

© 2005 by PRO-ED, Inc. All rights reserved. Duplicating this page is strictly prohibited.

3. What modifications could be implemented to provide Casey with access to the general education curriculum? Are there assistive technology interventions that could be effective for this child?

_____

_____

_____

_____

_____

_____

_____

4. Why are children with attentional problems prescribed stimulant medication? Are side effects such as Casey's common? Are these medications usually considered to be safe for children? Should teachers recommend medication for their students?

_____

_____

_____

_____

_____

_____

_____

5. Would it have been beneficial for Casey's parents to have followed through with the special education referral procedures through the school when Casey was initially referred in kindergarten? Why or why not?

_____

_____

_____

_____

_____

_____

_____

© 2005 by PRO-ED, Inc. All rights reserved. Duplicating this page is strictly prohibited.

CASE STUDIES

6. Create A Question (optional)

_____

_____

_____

_____

_____

_____

_____

David

David is a 13-year-old eighth grader at Heights Middle School. He was diagnosed as having a learning disability in the second grade. His primary learning difficulties currently include a fourth-grade reading level, extreme restlessness, and problems paying attention in class. Previously, he spent most of the instructional day in a special education classroom. This year, his parents, Mr. and Mrs. Hetzel, have made it clear to the school that they want David to be in the general education classroom throughout the entire day. They feel that the special education program has been too stigmatizing for their son. David has begun showing some symptoms of depression, which they believe are related to his special classroom placement. He has also started to talk about dropping out of school. For almost 3 years now, Mr. and Mrs. Hetzel have been trying to convince David's teachers that general education classroom placement is the most appropriate for his needs, particularly his social needs. David's teachers, however, have felt that the specialized instruction he receives in special education is preferable to the socialization experiences he may be missing. This year, Mr. and Mrs. Hetzel are seriously worried about David's depression, and they have told the school, in no uncertain terms, that there will be no more special classes for their son.

Background Information:

When David was diagnosed as having a learning disability in the second grade, he was also identified as having severe attention-deficit/hyperactivity disorder. This attentional problem, coupled with a significant reading disability, was considered to be a problem of such magnitude that it could only be treated in a self-contained special education setting. At the time of diagnosis, David was placed on medication for the hyperactivity and distractibility, but he experienced significant side effects and was taken off the medication. Another medication trial was attempted at the age of 10, but again the side effects resurfaced. It was determined that David could not safely tolerate any of the medications that typically control activity and attention problems in children. In the special education classroom, David's teachers were able to provide him with a very structured setting and considerable one-to-one instruction, which they knew he could not have received in the general education classroom.

Although Mr. and Mrs. Hetzel seem to be frustrated by David's slow progress in reading, his special education teachers see this progress as being significant. David's parents had hoped that all the intensive special education instruction would bring him up to grade level. Instead, they have seen the gap between

© 2005 by PRO-ED, Inc. All rights reserved. Duplicating this page is strictly prohibited.

grade placement and achievement widening every year since he began special education. This is disheartening enough for Mr. and Mrs. Hetzel, but now that David is experiencing emotional problems, they are starting to think that special education has been extremely detrimental to their child. The special education teachers view David's progress differently. They believe that David would be even further behind if he had not been provided with special education. They also believe that the social and emotional problems that David is now experiencing are nothing in comparison to the negative self-concept he would have if he had been left to fail year after year in a general education setting.

David's special education teachers are opposed to his being completely mainstreamed. They anticipate he will have many more problems in general education. In a one-to-one or small-group setting, David is able to fulfill work expectations, but in larger group situations where he does not get individual help, he tends to act out and be disruptive. In the past, teachers in classes in which he has been mainstreamed have viewed him as being disrespectful and causing behavior problems by not paying attention. They have suggested that David continue to receive special education services until he can demonstrate successful functioning in the mainstream.

 ## Case Study Activity

Individual Learning Plan

If David were assigned to your social studies class, describe how you would socially and academically integrate this student. In a two-page narrative, (a) identify what you consider to be David's four most important instructional and behavioral needs, (b) explain how you would address these identified needs with specific strategies for meeting social studies standards, (c) identify resources (e.g., teaching programs, Web resources, assistive technology, support personnel) that would provide assistance, and (d) describe how you would develop a systematic communication plan to keep the parents informed of progress.

_____

_____

_____

_____

_____

_____

_____

_____

_____

_____

© 2005 by PRO-ED, Inc. All rights reserved. Duplicating this page is strictly prohibited.

CASE STUDIES

© 2005 by PRO-ED, Inc. All rights reserved. Duplicating this page is strictly prohibited.

© 2005 by PRO-ED, Inc. All rights reserved. Duplicating this page is strictly prohibited.

CASE STUDIES

Jason

Jason is a 10-year-old third grader at Shores Elementary School. Last year, he was diagnosed as having a learning disability and attention-deficit/hyperactivity disorder. He is currently reading on a first-grade level. His auditory processing is so weak that he cannot use phonics for decoding purposes. He also has mild language comprehension problems that result in confusion with regard to his ability to follow classroom directions. His reading problems are complicated by his hyperactivity and distractibility. He can remain seated for a maximum of about 10 minutes at a time, and then only if he is in a room that is relatively free of distractions. He frequently gets out of his seat and wanders around the classroom. During this time, he often bothers other students by talking to them or showing them objects from his pocket. Verbal redirection is generally ineffective. The teacher has to come over to Jason, gently touch his shoulder or arm, and remind him that he should be in his seat working.

Jason has few friends. He is large for his age and, since he was retained once, he is considerably larger than his third-grade peers. Jason is considered to be the class clown who is always in trouble. His poor motor coordination causes him to frequently trip and fall. He also has a difficult time participating in playground activities. At recess, he usually wanders around the playground, sometimes spinning himself around until he gets dizzy. The other children consider him to be somewhat odd.

Background Information:

Jason was referred for special education evaluation during the first grade. The referral reasons included both academic and behavioral concerns. Jason's parents, Mr. and Mrs. Ballard, refused permission to evaluate. They asked the school to retain their son in first grade. They felt that because he was immature, another year might give him the added time to develop the academic and behavioral skills he was not demonstrating. When Jason showed little progress, Mr. and Mrs. Ballard decided to give permission for the evaluation. Jason's pediatrician took part in the evaluation and strongly recommended that Ritalin be prescribed to help Jason cope with the demands of the classroom. Jason's parents refused to consider this type of treatment. They are adamant in their position that medication not be included in the treatment plan for their son. They have agreed to let Jason receive special education services for 30 minutes per day in the resource room. He is to spend the rest of the instructional day in the general education classroom.

Case Study Activity

Individual Learning Plan

As Jason's third-grade teacher, describe how you would socially and academically integrate this student. In a two-page narrative, (a) identify what you consider to be Jason's four most important instructional and behavioral needs, (b) explain how you would address these identified needs with specific strategies for meeting the third-grade language arts standards, (c) identify resources (e.g., teaching programs, Web resources, assistive technology, support personnel) that would provide assistance, and (d) describe how you would develop a systematic communication plan to keep the parents informed of progress.

_____

_____

_____

© 2005 by PRO-ED, Inc. All rights reserved. Duplicating this page is strictly prohibited.

© 2005 by PRO-ED, Inc. All rights reserved. Duplicating this page is strictly prohibited.

CASE STUDIES

© 2005 by PRO-ED, Inc. All rights reserved. Duplicating this page is strictly prohibited.

Joseph

Joseph is a 6-year-old kindergarten student at Silver Maple Elementary School. He has been identified as having attention-deficit/hyperactivity disorder. The problems that this child presents in the classroom are inadequate readiness, hyperactivity, and distractibility. Whereas his classmates can sit in a circle for approximately 10 minutes at a time, Joseph can last for only a minute or two at the most. After that time has lapsed, he will invariably start grabbing at the other children, rolling around on the floor, making animal noises, or engaging in other distracting behaviors. In terms of readiness skills, he cannot identify the letters of the alphabet, he has a mild articulation problem, and he displays poor fine motor skills. Socially, he does not interact with his classmates unless one of them has a toy or game that he wants. In that case, he will grab it from the student and run away. If the other student resists, Joseph will use physical aggression to get his way. The kindergarten teacher has 24 children in this class with a paraprofessional who assists for 1 hour of the $2\frac{1}{2}$-hour day.

Background Information:

Joseph started kindergarten last fall and was taken out by his parents after 2 weeks of school. His teacher identified excessive activity level, impulsivity, and short attention span as problems that were precluding his successful adjustment to school. The kindergarten teacher and parents were in agreement that Joseph was too immature at that time to begin school. It was felt that, given another year, Joseph would be able to have a much more successful kindergarten experience. Now it is 2 weeks into the beginning of the school year and, much to the teacher's dismay, Joseph is demonstrating the very same behaviors that he did when he had previously started school.

Case Study Activity

Individual Learning Plan

As Joseph's kindergarten teacher, describe how you would socially and academically integrate this child into your classroom. In a two-page narrative, (a) identify what you consider to be Joseph's four most important instructional and behavioral needs, (b) explain how you would address these identified needs with specific strategies for meeting kindergarten language arts standards, (c) identify specific resources (e.g., teaching programs, Web resources, transition supports) that would provide assistance, and (d) describe how you would develop a systematic communication plan to keep the parents informed of progress.

_____

_____

_____

_____

_____

_____

_____

© 2005 by PRO-ED, Inc. All rights reserved. Duplicating this page is strictly prohibited.

© 2005 by PRO-ED, Inc. All rights reserved. Duplicating this page is strictly prohibited.

Attention Deficit with Hyperactivity Disorder

_____

_____

_____

_____

_____

_____

_____

_____

_____

_____

_____

_____

_____

_____

_____

_____

_____

_____

_____

Maria

Maria is a 9-year-old third grader at Oaktrail Elementary School. Her teacher, Mr. Hebert, feels that she is a low average student who does not have the motivation that some of his higher achieving third graders possess. He feels that she could do better than she is currently doing if she would spend less time day-dreaming and more time listening in class. However, she does not really cause any problems for him, so he is not especially concerned with her situation.

Maria's father, Mr. Salas, is very concerned about his daughter. He knows she is a bright child who is not achieving as she should be. Maria is receiving

© 2005 by PRO-ED, Inc. All rights reserved. Duplicating this page is strictly prohibited.

CASE STUDIES

Cs and Ds on her report cards. During the past two parent–teacher conferences, Mr. Salas expressed his concern about his daughter's progress to Mr. Hebert, who told him that Maria was not applying herself as well as she could be, but "that's the way some kids are." Mr. Salas asked if there was some way that Maria could get some extra help at school. Mr. Hebert told him that they did not have any special programs for increasing motivation, and he knew Maria would never qualify for special education services because she was not failing anything.

Background Information:

Maria is a physically beautiful child with long black hair and huge brown eyes. She has an ingratiating manner that many adults appreciate. When Maria was in preschool, the teacher told her parents that she believed Maria to be gifted in the area of art. Maria did exceptionally well in preschool because most of the curriculum was focused on visual–motor activities and socialization. During kindergarten, Maria was described as a "very capable student" who did well. The kindergarten teacher mentioned that Maria was usually not able to finish her work in the time allotted because of her daydreaming, but this was not a major concern because there was so much variation in kindergarten. In first grade, the teacher referred to Maria as "her wandering princess," saying that Maria had the habit of walking around the room to examine the bulletin board, book table, or contents of the wastepaper basket. This did not really bother the teacher because she felt that Maria was such a sweet child, and she could do the work when she got down to it. The first-grade teacher mentioned that she felt someday Maria would be a famous artist. However, she was concerned enough about Maria's poor listening habits to ask the school nurse to recheck her hearing and make sure that she did not have a loss that was not detected by the last school-wide hearing screening. By the time Maria began second grade, her grades started dropping, and the teacher started referring to "poor work habits," "weak listening skills," and "daydreaming" problems. Maria started to bring home work to finish at night that her classmates had finished during the day. Still, the teacher felt that Maria did not have major problems because "she didn't bother any of the other students."

Case Study Activity

Individual or Group Case Analysis

Answer the following questions and be prepared to discuss them in class.

1. Do you see any pattern in the teacher comments regarding Maria's behavior? Should Maria be referred for an attention-deficit disorder evaluation? Is it possible to have attentional problems without hyperactivity?

_____

_____

_____

_____

_____

_____

© 2005 by PRO-ED, Inc. All rights reserved. Duplicating this page is strictly prohibited.

2. Give four reasons why Maria's previous teachers have not identified a problem with her inattention.

_____

_____

_____

_____

_____

_____

3. Why does Mr. Hebert attribute Maria's problems to motivation? Do you think this type of attribution is common among teachers?

_____

_____

_____

_____

_____

_____

4. If Maria was referred for evaluation, do you think she would qualify for services? What laws might influence Maria's case?

_____

_____

_____

_____

_____

5. What curriculum factors and accommodations can you identify that might influence Maria's progress?

_____

_____

_____

_____

_____

© 2005 by PRO-ED, Inc. All rights reserved. Duplicating this page is strictly prohibited.

CASE STUDIES

6. Create A Question (optional)

_____

_____

_____

_____

_____

LeShawn

LeShawn is a 15-year-old at Southeast High School. He has been identified as having attention-deficit/hyperactivity disorder. He previously had significant difficulty with excessive activity level, causing him to be constantly moving around the room; however, he currently is struggling with extreme fidgetiness, restlessness, and impulsive behavior.

LeShawn's history class has been particularly difficult this semester. His teacher, Mr. Morton, uses the lecture format for this class. It is his expectation that all of his students conform to the rules. If they do not listen with respect and respond appropriately, he promptly issues a detention slip that requires the student to leave class and go to a special detention room. For every day that a student misses class without an excused absence, Mr. Morton subtracts one point from that student's final average for the class. Mr. Morton believes that his discipline plan has been tremendously successful. He is often asked by school officials to give talks about effective discipline practices at the high school level. He attributes the problem with discipline in the schools today to an absence of respect. He feels strongly that it is a sign of disrespect not to listen to the teacher and that students need to be shown that such behavior will not be tolerated. Mr. Morton believes there can be only one response to that kind of behavior: "The student must be excused from class, and he must pay the consequences of missing the work for that day." The principal, Mrs. Alphonse, backs him up 100 percent. She believes Mr. Morton is one of her best teachers, and she can always trust him to make the best decisions for the students and the school.

The problem in LeShawn's case is that, although he really likes history, he does not have the attention span for 50 minutes of a lecture class. About 10 minutes into class, he will start rocking in his chair, thumping out a beat on his desk, or fidgeting with his notes, book, or pencils. When this happens, Mr. Morton always gives him a warning: If he does not stop what he is doing, he will be sent to detention. That works for about 10 minutes, and then LeShawn will start shuffling his feet or cracking his knuckles. Mr. Morton will then calmly write out the detention slip and walk over to LeShawn's desk, continuing to lecture the whole time. Mr. Morton never raises his voice or gets angry. He believes that the most effective discipline plans are administered in a very calm, firm manner so that the student understands the consequences are not a matter of the teacher losing his temper, but rather of the student not living up to the expectations set for his class.

It is now 5 weeks into the fall semester, and LeShawn has already been issued 15 detention slips by Mr. Morton. He would have been issued more, but Mr. Morton was out with the flu for almost a full week. Although LeShawn is a bright student, it is unlikely that he is going to be able to pass Mr. Morton's class. He has already mentioned dropping out of school to his grandmother, Mrs. Gibbs, who is his guardian. LeShawn feels like there is no point in being

© 2005 by PRO-ED, Inc. All rights reserved. Duplicating this page is strictly prohibited.

in school if he is going to be failing most of his subjects. He feels that he could probably do better if he got a job. Mrs. Gibbs is very concerned, but she does not know what to do. She has diabetes, which has resulted in the amputation of both legs, and she is also losing her eyesight. It takes all of her energy to take care of LeShawn's laundry and meals. She does not have the physical strength to get on a bus and go down to the school to talk to his teachers. She has tried to complain to the principal, but Mrs. Alphonse told her that she is solidly behind Mr. Morton's discipline plan and that LeShawn needs to learn that off-task behaviors will not be tolerated.

Background Information:

LeShawn was taken away from his parents because of neglect when he was a preschooler. His parents are drug abusers who have been in and out of prison for drug-related convictions. He has lived with his elderly grandmother since the age of 3. LeShawn was referred to a pediatric neurologist by his social worker for possible lead poisoning at the age of 4. At that time, it

was determined that he had toxic levels of lead in his body, probably from eating paint chips. He was treated for several years for this toxicity. LeShawn was diagnosed as learning disabled with attention-deficit/hyperactivity disorder in the first grade. Medication was prescribed for the activity level problem, and he was placed in a self-contained classroom for the primary years. During the intermediate and middle school years, LeShawn attended resource classes. He continued to take his psychostimulant medication with good results. At the end of eighth grade, he was staffed out of special education because his progress had been considerable; he no longer met the requirements for special education services. About this time, it was discovered that LeShawn was selling his medication instead of using it himself. His social worker, grandmother, and doctor were in agreement: No more medication would be prescribed for LeShawn because of this problem and because he was doing so well in school. It was also thought that because LeShawn was an adolescent, he probably would not have as difficult a time controlling his activity level as he had in the past.

Case Study Activities

Part I:
Role Playing

Break into groups of four or five students and assume the roles of LeShawn, Mr. Morton, Mrs. Alphonse, Mr. Smithers (the Section 504 Building Coordinator, whose responsibility is to develop educational accommodation plans for students with disabilities), and Mrs. Gibbs (an optional role). Simulate a problem-solving conference in which these individuals attempt to find a resolution. Provide a written summary of the conference and its resolution.

Resolution

_____

_____

_____

_____

_____

© 2005 by PRO-ED, Inc. All rights reserved. Duplicating this page is strictly prohibited.

CASE STUDIES

Part II:
Individual or Group Case Analysis

Answer the following questions and be prepared to discuss them in class.

1. Could there be a relationship between LeShawn's past history of toxic lead levels and his attention and learning problems?

_____

_____

_____

_____

_____

_____

_____

2. Is Mr. Morton an effective teacher? From a legal perspective, does the school have the right to dismiss LeShawn from class on a routine basis for the behavior he is demonstrating? Why or why not?

_____

_____

_____

_____

_____

_____

3. What kinds of accommodations could be used in LeShawn's classes so that he could experience more success at school? What assistive technology supports might be beneficial to this student?

_____

_____

_____

_____

_____

_____

© 2005 by PRO-ED, Inc. All rights reserved. Duplicating this page is strictly prohibited.

4. Do most individuals "grow out" of attention-deficit disorder or should LeShawn be put back on his medication to help him be more successful? Is there any way to ensure that he will not resort to selling his medication again?

_____

_____

_____

_____

_____

_____

_____

5. What is the prognosis for LeShawn? Would LeShawn's outcome be different if he had a stronger advocate?

_____

_____

_____

_____

_____

_____

_____

6. Create A Question (optional)

_____

_____

_____

_____

_____

_____

_____

© 2005 by PRO-ED, Inc. All rights reserved. Duplicating this page is strictly prohibited.

CASE STUDIES

CHAPTER

Emotional/ Behavioral Disorders

Jody

Jody is a 9-year-old third-grade student at Gatesville Elementary School. Her teacher, Ms. Quioness, is quite concerned about her academic and social skills. Jody is a nonreader who appears to have very limited language skills. Although she can compute basic math facts, she has major deficits in reasoning and application of math skills. Ms. Quioness is even more concerned about social integration problems. Jody never smiles or talks to any of the other children, even when they ask her questions. Occasionally, she may shake or nod her head in response, but she rarely speaks. Jody cries frequently for no apparent reason. Ms. Quioness has the impression that the child is afraid to leave her side. Her desk is right next to the teacher's, and she remains there throughout the day. Ms. Quioness has to force her to go out to recess, where she stands next to the wall for the entire time. Jody also has a problem with enuresis; she wets herself almost every day. Ms. Quioness has never had a student such as this, and she is really at a loss about what to do for this child.

Background Information:

Jody was kidnapped by her father when she was 2 years old after a bitter divorce and custody battle. The father took both Jody and her 3-year-old brother from their mother, who had custody of the two children. For the past 7 years, Jody and her brother have had little contact with anyone but their father. For most of that time, the family was on the run to avoid the authorities. The father taught the children not to speak to anyone for fear that they would be taken away. He also told them that their mother had repeatedly abused them and would probably kill them if they were returned to her care. During this 7-year pe-riod, the children lived with their father in the car or in inexpensive motels. They basically roamed the country, staying mainly in rural areas to avoid detection. The children were discovered by the state police one chilly fall morning. The father had left them alone in the car for an evening of drinking. As he was making his way back to the car late at night, he apparently stumbled and fell into a ravine. After striking his head, he died of a cerebral hemorrhage. It was determined that the children were probably alone in the car for at least a day and a half before they were found by the police.

Although the mother had never given up hope that the children would one day be returned, she expressed uncertainty about integrating them into her new family once Jody and her brother were found. She had remarried 6 years ago, and she now has two other children with her second husband. Her husband has told the authorities that he believes the children would be better off with an adoptive family since they have been gone so long and are so fearful of their mother. Jody's mother has indicated to the teacher that she does not know what to do with the children. She describes Jody's behavior at home as being similar to what Ms. Quioness is observing at school, except at home Jody never leaves her brother's side and seems fearful of her mother and stepfather. It has been 2 months now since the children have been returned, and Jody's mother is beginning to wonder if her husband might be right about adoption. She loves her children, but she sometimes feels that her presence is causing their unhappiness. Things do not seem to be getting any better.

© 2005 by PRO-ED, Inc. All rights reserved. Duplicating this page is strictly prohibited.

CASE STUDIES

Case Study Activity

Individual or Group Case Analysis

Answer the following questions and be prepared to discuss them in class.

1. Should Ms. Quioness refer Jody for a special education evaluation? Why or why not?

_____

_____

_____

_____

_____

_____

2. Should Ms. Quioness be more concerned with Jody's socialization at this point or with her academic problems? Explain your response.

_____

_____

_____

_____

_____

_____

3. What kinds of strategies could Ms. Quioness use to encourage Jody to talk more? What kinds of strategies could Ms. Quioness use to encourage socialization opportunities for Jody?

_____

_____

_____

_____

_____

_____

© 2005 by PRO-ED, Inc. All rights reserved. Duplicating this page is strictly prohibited.

4. What should Ms. Quioness do about Jody's enuresis?

_____

_____

_____

_____

_____

_____

_____

5. If you were Ms. Quioness, would you attempt to provide assistance to this family? Why or why not? If you do think that you might be able to help, what types of resources might you use?

_____

_____

_____

_____

_____

_____

_____

6. Create A Question (optional)

_____

_____

_____

_____

_____

_____

_____

© 2005 by PRO-ED, Inc. All rights reserved. Duplicating this page is strictly prohibited.

CASE STUDIES

Joel

Joel is a 17-year-old adolescent at Kensington High School. He is a popular student at this private school, where he has been very active in athletics as well as social clubs. Last year, he was president of his class. This year, things are very different for this student. He has started missing quite a bit of school and has recently dropped the swim team and the chess club, two of his favorite extracurricular activities. In previous years, Joel was always at the center of a crowd of students, laughing and joking. This year, he frequently seems to be by himself. It is the first year he has not had a steady girlfriend. His grades have dropped from a 3.5 average to a 2.2.

Joel's math teacher, Mr. Dubois, who is also the advisor of the chess club, is disgusted with Joel's behavior. He has told other faculty members that Joel has probably gotten into the drug scene. Mr. Shaw, his history teacher and former swim team coach, thinks that Joel has just become lazy. He feels that a lot of kids from wealthy families such as Joel's have things too easy, so there is no motivation to keep striving for goals. Ms. Jardin, Joel's English teacher, does not agree with the other teachers. She has become increasingly disturbed by Joel's steady decline. She has noticed that while his manner of dress used to be impeccable, it now appears that he is wearing the same clothes over and over. Lately, it has occurred to Ms. Jardin that Joel is not bathing or observing other basic hygiene practices. When Ms. Jardin has carefully approached him about how things are going or how he is feeling, Joel has responded by telling her that he is tired because he has been studying too hard and staying up too late at night. Ms. Jardin knows this can hardly be true because the quality of his work has dropped dramatically.

Last week, an incident occurred that has caused Ms. Jardin to have additional concerns about Joel. A national news report about an adolescent suicide pact received quite a bit of media attention. During the same week, Joel wrote a theme on alienation and mentioned suicide as an alternative to "the day-to-day struggle to search for meaning in life." The mention of suicide in combination with Joel's behavior was enough to alarm Ms. Jardin. She called Joel's parents, Mr. and Mrs. Richert, to request a conference. Mr. Richert was on a business trip in Hong Kong, and Mrs. Richert was on a ski trip in Aspen. Ms. Jardin asked the housekeeper to have Mrs. Richert call her at her home number as soon as possible. Three days later, Mrs. Richert called Ms. Jardin at 11:30 P.M. When Ms. Jardin explained her concern for Joel and his mention of suicide, Mrs. Richert seemed to become irritated. She remarked that it was normal for teenagers to be depressed and that she herself had been depressed for all 4 years of high school. Mrs. Richert also mentioned that she was upset over Joel's latest report card, stating that if his teachers spent as much time worrying about his academics as they did worrying about his feelings, his grades might be a whole lot better. She then abruptly hung up.

Background Information:

Joel has always done extremely well in school, both academically and socially. He has never shown any symptoms of depression prior to this year. Joel is the only child of wealthy parents, who are very much involved in the community. Because his parents have such busy lives, he is alone with the housekeeper much of the time. Mr. and Mrs. Richert are proud of their son and his achievements. Mrs. Richert cannot help but notice that Joel is behaving differently, but she does not want to make a "big deal" about it. She is afraid that talking about depression will only make it worse. Her father committed suicide while he was being treated for depression. Mr. Richert, because of his busy schedule and traveling, is not really aware of any change in Joel.

© 2005 by PRO-ED, Inc. All rights reserved. Duplicating this page is strictly prohibited.

Case Study Activity

Individual or Group Case Analysis

Answer the following questions and be prepared to discuss them in class.

1. Has Ms. Jardin fulfilled her responsibilities by informing the parents of her concerns, or does she need to do more?

_____

_____

_____

_____

_____

_____

2. Do you think that encouraging adolescents to talk about their feelings regarding suicide increases the likelihood that they will attempt suicide? Why or why not?

_____

_____

_____

_____

_____

_____

3. Why do you think Joel's mother has responded in such a negative manner to Ms. Jardin's concerns? What kinds of events in her background may have influenced her response?

_____

_____

_____

_____

_____

_____

© 2005 by PRO-ED, Inc. All rights reserved. Duplicating this page is strictly prohibited.

4. Based on the information in this case study, do you think Joel's depression is severe or mild? Is there specific information in this case that leads you to this conclusion?

_____

_____

_____

_____

_____

_____

5. Other than identifying potential cases of suicide in their students and informing the parents and appropriate school personnel, is there anything else that secondary education teachers can do to help students who are dealing with significant bouts of depression?

_____

_____

_____

_____

_____

_____

6. Create A Question (optional)

_____

_____

_____

_____

_____

_____

© 2005 by PRO-ED, Inc. All rights reserved. Duplicating this page is strictly prohibited.

Levonda

Levonda is a 6-year-old first grader at Willowbrook Elementary School. She spent her kindergarten year in a preschool program for children with special needs. Levonda's diagnosis of emotional disturbance was based on her extreme withdrawal resulting from a pattern of sexual abuse, which this child endured for an extended period of time. Levonda also developed a phobia of school, making it very difficult for her to separate from her mother, Mrs. Rand. Although Levonda is still considered to be a very disturbed child, her special education teacher, Mrs. Holmes, feels that her needs could be met in the general education classroom environment because she does not have academic problems. Mrs. Holmes has so many children with autism in her classroom that she feels Levonda will not be provided with the type of role models that would help her to learn appropriate social skills. She strongly recommended that Levonda be placed into a first-grade general education classroom.

Levonda's first-grade teacher, Ms. Chinn, is an energetic young woman in her first year of teaching. When her principal told her that Levonda would be included in her class, Ms. Chinn was not upset. In fact, she felt complimented that the principal, Mrs. Shapiro, would give her such a challenging child to work with during her first year in the classroom. Ms. Chinn took it as a vote of confidence from her administrator. She looked forward to meeting Levonda and helping her work through some of her problems.

On the first day of school, Ms. Chinn met Levonda and Mrs. Rand at the front door. In her softest and most reassuring voice, Ms. Chinn told her how happy she was that Levonda would be one of her students, and then she gently picked up Levonda's hand to walk her to her desk. As soon as she touched Levonda's hand, Levonda began to scream in a loud, high-pitched voice. Ms. Chinn immediately dropped her hand and Levonda ran to her mother, continuing to scream for the next 5 minutes. Ms. Chinn was very upset, but she tried to compose herself to greet the other students. When Levonda finally stopped screaming, her mother firmly told her that it was time for her to leave, but that she would be back after school. Levonda started to scream again, so Mrs. Rand asked Ms. Chinn to hold her until she left the building. As Ms. Chinn restrained Levonda, she began to cry and scream louder. She also started kicking Ms. Chinn. At this point, some of the other first graders began to cry. The principal walked by the classroom and came in with a very concerned look on her face and said, "Ms. Chinn, please get this situation under control!"

After about 10 minutes, Levonda's screams were reduced to sobs and quiet whimpering. She found her way to a corner and stayed there for the next hour. Ms. Chinn decided to leave her alone a while, hoping that she would slowly adjust to the classroom in her own way. However, Ms. Chinn could not ignore the fact that Levonda had picked up a rag doll in the book corner and had begun masturbating with it. Levonda had pulled her dress up and was thrusting the rag doll in such a fashion as to attract attention, and many of her classmates had noticed the commotion in the book corner. Ms. Chinn got up from her desk and took the doll from Levonda and pulled down her dress. Levonda began screaming again. It took her 15 minutes to settle down this time.

Ms. Chinn is seriously considering resignation. The only peace she has in her first-grade classroom is when Levonda is with Mrs. Holmes for an hour and 15 minutes in the afternoon. Levonda's special education teacher is sympathetic about the first-grade classroom situation, but she really feels that Levonda just needs more time with typical peers. "It will get better for you and Levonda," Mrs. Holmes says. Ms. Chinn has no reason to believe this is true. In the 4 weeks that Levonda has been with Ms. Chinn, her pattern of behavior remains the same on a daily basis. Every morning she cries loudly and has to be restrained when her mother leaves. She stays in the corner and refuses to be part of the class, screaming when Ms. Chinn or her classmates try to approach her. Ms. Chinn cannot get her interested in any of the first-grade activities, and Levonda seems intent on spending much of her time masturbating in the book corner or at her desk. The principal recently told Ms. Chinn that she has had a number of complaints from parents, and she suggested that some significant changes be made so that this first-grade classroom is a more comfortable place for all the children. Ms. Chinn has no idea how to accomplish this.

© 2005 by PRO-ED, Inc. All rights reserved. Duplicating this page is strictly prohibited.

CASE STUDIES

Background Information:

When Levonda started preschool at the age of 3, Mrs. Rand would drop her off on her way to work. Mr. Rand would then pick her up from preschool, as he was unemployed. He was in charge of Levonda's afternoon care. It was during this time period that Levonda began having behavior problems. A routine visit to the pediatrician revealed that Levonda had been sexually abused, and a social worker was called in to help the family. Levonda's father left the home and entered a counseling program. He came back into the home after he had successfully completed the program. A year later, another routine visit to the pediatrician revealed that, once again, Levonda was being sexually abused. This time, Mrs. Rand divorced Mr. Rand, but Levonda's behavior had deteriorated to the point that the social worker referred her to Child Find. She was diagnosed as seriously emotionally disturbed with extreme withdrawal, separation anxiety, tactile defensiveness, and depressive symptoms. Full-time, special education programming was recommended for her kindergarten school year.

 Case Study Activity

Individual or Group Case Analysis

Answer the following questions and be prepared to discuss them in class.

1. Why is Levonda having such a difficult time separating from her mother? What strategies should Ms. Chinn try to help her with this separation? Is physical restraint an appropriate strategy in this situation?

_____

_____

_____

_____

_____

2. Is it the principal's responsibility to assist the teachers with management problems such as these, or should teachers be responsible for all student management problems?

_____

_____

_____

_____

_____

_____

_____

© 2005 by PRO-ED, Inc. All rights reserved. Duplicating this page is strictly prohibited.

3. What should Ms. Chinn do about Levonda's masturbation? How can she address the problem of tactile defensiveness with this child? What resources might Ms. Chinn use to help her with Levonda?

_____

_____

_____

_____

_____

_____

_____

4. Should Levonda be in a general education first-grade classroom such as Ms. Chinn's, or could she be better served in Mrs. Holmes' classroom with the autistic children? Were appropriate transition supports implemented when Levonda was moved from the special education preschool to her kindergarten classroom?

_____

_____

_____

_____

_____

_____

_____

5. What should Ms. Chinn do about the other parents' complaints?

_____

_____

_____

_____

_____

_____

_____

© 2005 by PRO-ED, Inc. All rights reserved. Duplicating this page is strictly prohibited.

CASE STUDIES

6. Create A Question (optional)

_____

_____

_____

_____

_____

_____

_____

_____

Miguel

Miguel is a 10-year-old fifth grader at Meadowview Elementary. He was diagnosed with emotional disturbance when he was in third grade. At that time, he was placed in a self-contained classroom where he stayed for 2 years. This year, Miguel has been assigned to Mr. Rivera's fifth-grade class because of the school district's move toward more inclusive environments for students with disabilities. He was considered to be a good candidate for the move to a general classroom because his reading and math skills are only a year below grade level, which is substantially higher than that of his peers in the self-contained special education classroom. It has been 2 weeks since the beginning of the school year, and Mr. Rivera is perplexed about the situation in his classroom. Initially, he was not opposed to having Miguel in his classroom, even though other teachers made comments and rolled their eyes whenever the principal referred to the placement change for Miguel. Mr. Rivera views himself as a "take charge" kind of teacher who enjoys the challenges that his students present to him. Now, he is having second thoughts about Miguel's place in his classroom.

Miguel has many positive qualities that Mr. Rivera tries to focus on and reinforce. He is a kind child with a gentle, sensitive nature and a good sense of humor (when he is feeling well). However, Miguel

also has many troublesome behaviors that seem to get more attention than his positive behaviors. One example of these behaviors is Miguel's persistence in turning statements around to negate whatever is being said. For example, when Sara's mother came to pick her up for a dentist's appointment one day, Miguel saw her at the door and immediately began calling out, "Sara, that is _not_ your mother. I know for a fact that woman is not your mother." He does the same thing in class with whatever facts Mr. Rivera is trying to teach, such as states and their capitals. All of a sudden, he will call out, "Springfield is _not_ the capital of Illinois!" When Mr. Rivera tries to reason with him, Miguel tearfully defends his actions by saying, "Mr. Rivera, I really like you, but I cannot let you lie to all these students." And he will persist even when shown a map of the states with the capitals written on it. "The people who made this map are lying!" he will insist. Mr. Rivera tries to ignore this behavior, but it is difficult to do because it is so disruptive.

The most troublesome aspect of having Miguel in the classroom is his persistent self-abusive behavior. Miguel frequently uses pens, pencils, rulers, or other objects to cut the inside of his forearms. This happens several times a day, usually when Mr. Rivera is helping another student. Miguel will begin by running the pen or pencil lightly up and down his arm, and then he

© 2005 by PRO-ED, Inc. All rights reserved. Duplicating this page is strictly prohibited.

will gradually increase the pressure until he begins bleeding. When he is engaging in this injurious behavior, he gets a glazed expression on his face. Sometimes, Mr. Rivera does not even know it is happening until one of his students tells him that "Miguel is at it again." He will then run over and take the object away. Usually after cutting himself, Miguel seems to be more relaxed. It is as if the injury provides him with some kind of psychological relief. Miguel often has to be taken to the nurse's office for first aid. Once, he had to be taken to the hospital because he had cut into an artery. This behavior is frustrating for Mr. Rivera because he feels that he has to watch Miguel every minute or he will hurt himself. He thinks that his other 25 students are being neglected because he has to give so much attention to Miguel. He is starting to worry that his class will do poorly on the state assessments, which will be interpreted as a reflection of his inability to address the prescribed curriculum. Mr. Rivera is also starting to lose some confidence in his ability to handle his classroom, which really depresses him. He has always enjoyed teaching, but this year he is starting to dread many days.

Background Information:

Miguel was 8 years old when he witnessed his father shoot his pregnant mother and baby sister to death in an incident of domestic violence. Since the shooting, he has suffered severe emotional distress that has been manifested in self-injurious behavior and mutism. For 1 full year after his mother's death, Miguel did not utter a word. He and his three surviving brothers were put into separate foster homes. It was later uncovered that Miguel's first foster father sexually abused him repeatedly. No one knew at the time because he was not speaking. Miguel was in that abusive home for a year when the foster family abruptly left town without any explanation to the authorities. Miguel was left alone in the rented house with another foster child for 2 days before the landlord discovered that the family had abandoned them. Miguel was transferred to another foster care family, where he stayed for 6 months. It was during this time that he began to talk and physically abuse himself. The foster family asked that Miguel be removed because they could not deal with the self-injurious behavior. Miguel now lives in a group home.

Case Study Activity

Individual or Group Case Analysis

Answer the following questions and be prepared to discuss them in class.

1. Should Miguel be placed in a self-contained special education classroom? Why or why not? Do you think the other students in Mr. Rivera's class are suffering because of the inclusion of Miguel? Is there a solution for balancing the rights of nondisabled students and the rights of disabled students who need access to the curriculum?

_____

_____

_____

_____

_____

_____

© 2005 by PRO-ED, Inc. All rights reserved. Duplicating this page is strictly prohibited.

2. Why do you think Miguel injures himself? What should Mr. Rivera do about Miguel's self-injurious behavior? Explain four specific strategies that you would use to decrease this behavior if you were his teacher.

_____

_____

_____

_____

_____

_____

3. What strategies should Mr. Rivera use to decrease Miguel's odd behavior of negating facts?

_____

_____

_____

_____

_____

_____

4. What is the prognosis for Miguel? Can you think of any factors that could enhance this prognosis?

_____

_____

_____

_____

_____

_____

5. What kinds of strategies can Mr. Rivera use to relieve his stress and start to get his confidence back?

_____

_____

_____

_____

_____

_____

© 2005 by PRO-ED, Inc. All rights reserved. Duplicating this page is strictly prohibited.

6. Create A Question (optional)

_____

_____

_____

_____

_____

_____

Mitchell

Mitchell is an 11-year-old fourth grader at Alameda Elementary School. He was identified as having a serious emotional disturbance at the age of 7. Since that time, he has been in a self-contained classroom for students with behavioral disorders.

This morning, when he was standing in line waiting to enter the school building, he was involved in an altercation with a second-grade child. During the fight, Mitchell pulled a rubber knife out of his back pocket and began stabbing the other boy. Because the knife was a toy, the second grader was not hurt, but the effect of the incident was horrifying to the children who were observing the fight and to the teachers who broke it up. The principal, Mr. Reid, called Mitchell's mother, Mrs. Fazano, and told her to come and get her child immediately, as he was expelled for the remainder of the school year. The school district has a policy of expelling all students who bring weapons or facsimiles of weapons to school.

Mrs. Fazano is outraged that her son is being expelled. She has had numerous disagreements with Mr. Reid in the past as a result of the way he has disciplined Mitchell. She feels that her son receives punishment that is much more severe than what the other children receive for the same infractions. Mrs. Fazano is also upset because she has no childcare for Mitchell, and she cannot afford to pay anyone to supervise him. She has just been hired at a new job that she feels is really going to work out for her, but she knows she will not be able to keep it if Mitchell is not in school. Mrs. Fazano is going to call the Legal Aid Advocacy Center for Children with Disabilities and try to get some help.

Background Information:

When Mitchell was initially identified as having an emotional disturbance, the pupil assessment report described him as a "deeply troubled child who has demonstrated a marked pattern of physical and verbal aggression over an extended period of time." The report recommended that Mitchell's behavior required a self-contained setting in which he could be provided the necessary support for his disability, support which he needed to develop anger control strategies. Unfortunately, the special education classroom has not been able to provide Mitchell with the assistance that was recommended. Since he started in this program in the second grade, he has had 12 different teachers. Most of these teachers were not certified in the area in which they were teaching. They were hired as substitutes or temporary teachers until a fully certified special education teacher could be found. Alameda Elementary is in a low socioeconomic area of the city that has major problems with crime. It is difficult to attract any teachers, much less those who are interested and trained in the area of emotional disturbance. Alameda's program for students with emotional disturbance serves students who have some of the most serious problems in the school district, and many of these problems are manifested in aggressive behavior.

Mr. Reid is very familiar with Mitchell because he is frequently sent down to his office for incidents

© 2005 by PRO-ED, Inc. All rights reserved. Duplicating this page is strictly prohibited.

related to uncontrollable behavior. The principal knows that many of Mitchell's school problems are due to inadequacies in his special education program. He wishes he could find a good special education teacher for that classroom. He knows it would make his job a lot easier. He also feels that Mitchell's mother is partly to blame because she does not seem to have any control over his behavior at home or at school. Mr. Reid has been the principal at Alameda for more years than he would like to count, and he is starting to feel worn down by the problems of the community. He would like to see parents take responsibility for their children's problems instead of leaving everything to the schools. He is glad that he can call Mrs. Lu, the school district's discipline officer, in case Mrs. Fazano creates a commotion about this expulsion. Mrs. Lu really knows how to play "hard ball" with the parents of hard-to-handle kids.

Case Study Activities

Part I: Role Playing

Break into groups of four with each student assuming one of the following roles: Mr. Reid, Mrs. Fazano, Mr. Montoya (attorney for Legal Aid Advocacy Center for Children with Disabilities), and Mrs. Lu. Simulate a problem-solving meeting whereby these individuals attempt to reach a resolution for this case. Summarize the results of this meeting.

Resolution

_____

_____

_____

_____

_____

_____

_____

_____

_____

_____

_____

© 2005 by PRO-ED, Inc. All rights reserved. Duplicating this page is strictly prohibited.

Part II:
Individual or Group Case Analysis

Answer the following questions and be prepared to discuss them in class.

1. Does the school have the legal right to expel this child? Why or why not? What laws might influence this case?

_____

_____

_____

_____

_____

_____

2. What do you think should be done for Mitchell? Should he be allowed to stay at this school, should he be expelled, or should he be transferred to another school? Explain your answer.

_____

_____

_____

_____

_____

_____

3. Has Mitchell received an appropriate education at Alameda Elementary? Explain your answer.

_____

_____

_____

_____

_____

_____

© 2005 by PRO-ED, Inc. All rights reserved. Duplicating this page is strictly prohibited.

CASE STUDIES

4. In your opinion, what can be done to attract teachers to assume challenging positions at schools such as Alameda?

_____

_____

_____

_____

_____

_____

_____

5. If you were Mitchell's teacher, how would you work with Mrs. Fazano to establish a home–school behavior management plan? What would be some of the essential features of this plan? Identify some of the possible constraints you would have in working with this parent, and describe how you would overcome these.

_____

_____

_____

_____

_____

_____

6. Create A Question (optional)

_____

_____

_____

_____

_____

_____

_____

© 2005 by PRO-ED, Inc. All rights reserved. Duplicating this page is strictly prohibited.

Rinna

Rinna is a 5-year-old who started kindergarten at Crawford Elementary School 2 weeks ago. She has been diagnosed with emotional disturbance. This child has never had any preschool experience nor any interaction with other children. In addition to emotional problems, Rinna has delayed language and readiness skills. She confuses colors and cannot consistently identify shapes. She does not know the alphabet or number concepts past 3. Rinna has difficulty holding crayons and pencils for writing purposes. Over the years, Mrs. Vasquez, the kindergarten teacher, has had experience teaching many students who are not prepared to meet school expectations, but Rinna's problems are far more troubling because of her behavioral difficulties.

Whenever Rinna becomes the least bit frustrated or tired, she pretends that she is a dog. She gets down on her hands and knees and begins barking in an animated fashion. Rinna also licks the floor, furniture, and any children in her immediate vicinity. Most of the kindergarten students think this behavior is uproariously funny, except for the ones who are being licked, many of whom end up in tears. Rinna will not respond to redirection or to Mrs. Vasquez's requests to stop the behavior. The only way that Mrs. Vasquez has been able to stop the behavior is by literally chasing Rinna around the room until she catches her. Eventually, Rinna ends up in tears when Mrs. Vasquez finally gets her to stop. She will often continue to cry loudly for about 10 minutes, usually screaming, "You hate me—I hate you, too—I hate all of you!" Obviously, this has an unsettling impact on the rest of the kindergartners. Because Rinna has limited readiness skills, she is frustrated for most of the time she is working on her kindergarten curriculum. The only part of the morning that does not seem upsetting for her is the time she spends with Mr. Asante, the special education teacher who comes into Mrs. Vasquez's class for 30 minutes each day. During this time, Rinna seldom exhibits any of the bizarre behavior that characterizes the remainder of the kindergarten morning.

Mrs. Vasquez is a 15-year veteran kindergarten teacher who is feeling completely overwhelmed by this 5-year-old. Last week, two angry parents called the principal with complaints regarding Rinna's licking behavior. The principal told Mrs. Vasquez that she had better "get the situation under control immediately." Mrs. Vasquez is well aware of the problems in her classroom. She knows that her kindergarten students are not learning what they need to be learning because of the distraction of Rinna's behavior. She is very concerned that her kindergartners are 3 weeks behind in their curriculum. This year, it is taking much longer to meet the district's instructional standards because of the time she spends controlling Rinna's behavior. Meeting the curriculum standards has always been a priority with Mrs. Vasquez. It bothers her that she does not feel as if she is in control of the situation. She is wondering if she has lost her skills as a kindergarten teacher.

Background Information:

From birth to age $2\frac{1}{2}$, Rinna was cared for mainly by her maternal grandmother who lived with the family. This childcare situation was necessitated by the fact that Rinna's mother, Mrs. Bessant, was a very disturbed woman who suffered from manic–depressive illness. Rinna was well cared for by her grandmother until the woman died suddenly of a stroke. From that time on, she was cared for by her mother. However, Mrs. Bessant was so ill that she simply could not meet her child's daily needs. Every day, she put Rinna out in a fenced yard with two family dogs. Rinna would stay in the yard all day long, eating and drinking out of the dog dishes until her father would return from the fields. He would bring her in, clean her up, and put her to bed. Because he was a farmer, he was in the fields from sunup to sunset on most days. On occasions, when he came in early because of rain, he would find Rinna in the doghouse. When he questioned his wife about it, she would tell him that she tried to get Rinna to come in the house but the child would not leave the company of her pets. Mr. Bessant knew that the childcare situation was not satisfactory, but he did not know the extent of the neglect. His growing uneasiness, coupled with Rinna's slow development, prompted him to ask his mother to come and live with them so that she could assist in the care of both his wife and daughter. Just before she arrived, Mrs. Bessant committed suicide.

When the paternal grandmother moved in, she knew immediately that something was drastically wrong with her grandchild. She convinced her son to

© 2005 by PRO-ED, Inc. All rights reserved. Duplicating this page is strictly prohibited.

CASE STUDIES

take Rinna to the pediatrician, who told them that he had not seen her since she was 6 months old. Mr. Bessant was aghast because he had questioned his wife numerous times about the pediatrician's opinion of Rinna's development. The pediatrician referred the family to the state medical university 200 miles away, where Rinna received a comprehensive evaluation and a diagnosis of emotional disturbance. Mr. Bessant was overcome with guilt when the psychologist informed him of Rinna's description of life under the care of her mother. He feels that he is responsible for Rinna's condition because he did not get her the proper care she needed. The evaluation team at the hospital recommended that Rinna attend the residential psychiatric kindergarten school program at the hospital, where she would have the benefit of an intensive treatment plan that would not be possible in other settings. Both Mr. Bessant and his mother were adamant in their feeling that Rinna needed to come home to be cared for, so they could try to make up for the past neglect. They feel that given time and a lot of loving care, Rinna will once again become "well."

Case Study Activity

Individual or Group Case Analysis

Answer the following questions and be prepared to discuss them in class.

1. Does Rinna's diagnosis of emotional disturbance influence the type of methods that Mrs. Vasquez will use to teach her readiness skills? Why or why not?

_____

_____

_____

_____

_____

_____

2. What can Mrs. Vasquez do about Rinna's classroom behavior? Identify two long-term behavior goals and describe how these could be addressed in a behavior management plan that could be used in this situation.

_____

_____

_____

_____

_____

_____

© 2005 by PRO-ED, Inc. All rights reserved. Duplicating this page is strictly prohibited.

3. While Mrs. Vasquez is working on a plan for Rinna's behavior, what can she do to help the other children to adjust to the classroom situation? How can she handle complaints from parents?

_____

_____

_____

_____

_____

_____

_____

_____

4. What transition supports should have been put into place to assist this student and teacher? Identify at least three and explain how they could have enhanced the kindergarten learning environment.

_____

_____

_____

_____

_____

_____

_____

_____

5. Does Rinna belong in Mrs. Vasquez's kindergarten class? Does she belong in the psychiatric kindergarten at the state hospital? Support your opinion for the most appropriate placement for this child.

_____

_____

_____

_____

_____

_____

_____

_____

© 2005 by PRO-ED, Inc. All rights reserved. Duplicating this page is strictly prohibited.

CASE STUDIES

6. Create A Question (optional)

_____

_____

_____

_____

_____

_____

_____

© 2005 by PRO-ED, Inc. All rights reserved. Duplicating this page is strictly prohibited.

Emotional/Behavioral Disorders

CHAPTER 5

Physical Disabilities and Health Impairments

Chad

Chad is a 12-year-old sixth grader at Daniels Middle School. He was diagnosed with acute lymphoblastic leukemia at the age of 7. Since this time, he has been in and out of remission. He has recently had a relapse that required intensive chemotherapy and caused him to lose all of his hair. Chad has mild learning disabilities in the areas of reading and math. He also struggles with subtle language processing difficulties and problems with short-term memory. It is believed that these learning problems are related to the intensive chemotherapy that he has endured to combat the cancer. Mr. Chong, his English teacher, has previously been concerned about Chad's achievement, but he has started to become more concerned about Chad's withdrawn behavior. Chad has stopped participating in class, and he is not doing any homework. He generally keeps his head down on the desk during English class or stares out the window. When Mr. Chong tries to include him in discussion, he seldom answers but just shrugs his shoulders, keeping his eyes fixed on his shoes.

Mr. Chong has shared his concern with Mrs. Hafstrom, Chad's learning disabilities teacher. Mrs. Hafstrom is also worried about Chad. During the 50 minutes per day that he attends her learning lab, he seems distant and preoccupied. Mrs. Hafstrom believes that he is very depressed about his illness. When she questions him about how he is feeling, he frequently makes off-hand remarks, such as "Pretty good for a kid who's headed for the grave," or "I'm feeling kind of down, like six feet under." This kind of talk alienates Chad from his peers, who avoid him more and more frequently. Mrs. Hafstrom believes that Chad is a very depressed child who needs help, but she is uncertain of how to go about providing this assistance to him.

Background Information:

During the last IEP meeting, Mrs. Hafstrom requested that Chad be invited to participate in setting goals. Chad's mother, Mrs. Kelly, told her that his inclusion was "absolutely out of the question." At the meeting, Mr. and Mrs. Kelly told the pupil assessment team that they did not want Chad to be present because they wanted to talk about the prognosis of his illness. They related how Chad's oncologist had told them that Chad would probably die sometime this year. His doctor believes that there will not be another remission of the cancer. Mrs. Kelly tearfully told the team that she wanted Chad to have the best year possible without him having to worry about the seriousness of his illness. In spite of the doctor's recommendation that Chad be informed of the prognosis, Mr. and Mrs. Kelly believe that no purpose can be served by giving him this information. It was obvious to all the assessment team members who were present that both parents were in such a state of grief that they could not look at other alternatives for helping Chad face his illness. At the close of the IEP meeting, Mrs. Kelly made it clear that she did not want any teacher or psychologist to discuss the issue of death with Chad. Both parents insisted that the IEP goals should address only academic needs and the family would deal with the affective needs.

© 2005 by PRO-ED, Inc. All rights reserved. Duplicating this page is strictly prohibited.

CASE STUDIES

Case Study Activity

Individual or Group Case Analysis

Answer the following questions and be prepared to discuss them in class.

1. Do you think Chad knows what his prognosis is? Should he be told? Explain your position.

_____

_____

_____

_____

_____

_____

_____

2. If you were Mr. Chong, what would you do in English class to increase Chad's participation?

_____

_____

_____

_____

_____

_____

3. If you were Mrs. Hafstrom, how would you help meet Chad's affective needs given the restrictions the parents have placed on you?

_____

_____

_____

_____

_____

_____

© 2005 by PRO-ED, Inc. All rights reserved. Duplicating this page is strictly prohibited.

4. Should students with disabilities typically be present at their IEP meetings, or is it a good idea to exclude them, particularly when information of a sensitive nature is going to be discussed? Explain your position.

_____

_____

_____

_____

_____

_____

_____

5. As a teacher, can you think of any other ways you might be able to assist this family?

_____

_____

_____

_____

_____

_____

_____

6. Create A Question (optional)

_____

_____

_____

_____

_____

_____

_____

© 2005 by PRO-ED, Inc. All rights reserved. Duplicating this page is strictly prohibited.

CASE STUDIES

Janell

Janell is a 10-year-old child in the fourth grade at Wheeling Elementary School. She uses a wheelchair because she is paralyzed from the lumbar region down as a result of spina bifida. Janell also has learning disabilities that her doctor believes are the result of hydrocephalus, a condition with which she was born. Janell's brain was shunted immediately after her birth, and she has not experienced problems since that time. She is in a general education classroom for the entire day, but she receives reading assistance from a special education teacher, Mrs. Kirchmar, who works with her for 30 minutes per day in her general education classroom. Janell has recurrent seizures that are controlled by Dilantin. She experiences swollen and bleeding gums as a side effect of this medication. Janell has vision problems, including strabismus and refractive errors that require very thick corrective lenses. Although she has had three eye surgeries, the strabismus is still readily apparent.

Janell has considerable difficulty with her school work, but both her fourth-grade and special education teachers are very supportive. They have recently become increasingly concerned because Janell appears to be becoming more and more withdrawn. She does not seem to have any friends and lately, Mrs. Bowman, her general education teacher, has noticed that she is becoming the object of classroom jokes. Many of these jokes are focused on her physical appearance, such as her crossed eyes, her weight (Janell weighs 130 pounds), and even her wheelchair. Mrs. Bowman is starting to think that maybe Janell would be happier in a special education setting where "she could be friends with other children who are confined to wheelchairs." Mrs. Kirchmar does not agree that a special education classroom is the answer for Janell, but she does agree that Janell is unhappy in her current school situation. Both teachers have attempted to get Mr. Metz, Janell's father, to come to school for a parent–teacher conference to discuss these concerns, but he has politely declined on numerous occasions. Finally, out of frustration, Mrs. Bowman and Mrs. Kirchmar went to see Mr. Metz at home in the evening. Mr. Metz would not let the teachers come into his home. He stood at the door and stated that he was not interested in discussing any of Janell's school difficulties because he had made the decision to place her in Roseman School, a residential school that serves children with severe disabilities. It has a reputation as a dismal institution where children are typically neglected. Both teachers were shocked to hear this news. When Mrs. Kirchmar asked him if they could come in just for a few minutes to talk about Roseman, Mr. Metz said, "No, I'm sorry—there's nothing more to talk about."

Background Information:

Janell's father is a widower whose wife died of cancer when Janell was 3 years old. Since that time, Mr. Metz relied on an elderly neighbor to assist him in the care of Janell. This woman, Miss Shaw, had taken on all of the major responsibilities for this child. Miss Shaw bought Janell's clothes, dressed her, made all of her meals, and helped her with homework and school projects. Miss Shaw was the family's only outside contact, as they live a reclusive life. Miss Shaw came over to Janell's house at 7:00 every morning when Mr. Metz left for work and stayed until 8:00 in the evening when he returned. This routine continued for 7 years until last month, when Miss Shaw fell as she was lifting Janell from her bed into her wheelchair. She broke her hip bone and ended up in the hospital. Miss Shaw's relatives have informed Mr. Metz that she will not be returning to her home because she will be living in a retirement home when she leaves the hospital.

© 2005 by PRO-ED, Inc. All rights reserved. Duplicating this page is strictly prohibited.

Case Study Activity

Individual or Group Case Analysis

Answer the following questions and be prepared to discuss them in class.

1. What do you think is the reason for Janell's withdrawal? If you were Mrs. Bowman, what would you do to increase Janell's socialization opportunities in the general education classroom? How would you deal with the jokes that are made by her peers?

_____

_____

_____

_____

_____

_____

2. Why do you think Mr. Metz refused to come to the school for a conference? Do you think it was a good idea for Janell's teachers to make a home visit? Are there other strategies that teachers can use to communicate with parents who are difficult to reach?

_____

_____

_____

_____

_____

_____

3. Why would Janell's father want to put his daughter in a residential school that serves children with severe physical and mental disabilities?

_____

_____

_____

_____

_____

© 2005 by PRO-ED, Inc. All rights reserved. Duplicating this page is strictly prohibited.

4. Why do you think Mrs. Bowman believes that Janell would be happier in a special education placement? Do you agree or disagree? Explain your position.

_____

_____

_____

_____

_____

_____

_____

_____

5. Is there anything these teachers can do to stop Mr. Metz from putting Janell in this residential school?

_____

_____

_____

_____

_____

_____

_____

_____

6. Create A Question (optional)

_____

_____

_____

_____

_____

_____

_____

_____

© 2005 by PRO-ED, Inc. All rights reserved. Duplicating this page is strictly prohibited.

Melissa

Melissa is a 13-year-old student in the eighth grade at Spencer Middle School. She is a very attractive adolescent who has been enormously popular among students and teachers alike since she started here in sixth grade. Last summer, Melissa was involved in a bicycle accident that resulted in a closed head injury. Although Melissa is progressing very well considering the injury, her family has been told that it will take quite a while for her to fully recover. The doctors have also mentioned the possibility that Melissa may never have the same motor coordination that she had possessed prior to the accident. The most pressing concern for the family now is dealing with Melissa's seizure disorder, which has developed as a result of the head injury. Melissa now experiences tonic-clonic seizures on a weekly basis. Although a number of medications have been tried, they have not yet successfully controlled her seizures. Melissa's doctors hope that they will eventually be able to control these seizures, but for the time being they have told the family that they must be prepared to deal with them as they occur.

Melissa's parents, Mr. and Mrs. Zemke, have been working with the staff at Spencer to ensure that Melissa's needs are accommodated. Initially, they felt the school was very responsive to their requests, but lately they have had second thoughts. They are starting to wonder if they should hire an attorney to impress upon the school the necessity of the modifications they have requested. The major disagreement that has arisen is a result of differences regarding seizure management. Melissa's neurologist has emphasized the importance of preventing any secondary brain damage that might result from a fall during a seizure. The Zemkes have asked that Melissa's peers be trained in seizure management so that when Melissa starts to have a seizure, her peers can catch her and prevent her from hitting her head on a desk or the floor. The school does not agree with this request. The principal, Mrs. Gust, on the advice of the school nurse, has recommended that Melissa wear a helmet during the day to protect her head in case of a fall from a seizure. When Mrs. Zemke heard this, she was extremely upset. The idea of her daughter wearing a helmet around school all day, calling attention to her problems, was simply ludicrous to her.

Mrs. Gust has argued that it does not seem reasonable to expect Melissa's peers to be responsible for preventing secondary brain damage. She mentioned to the Zemkes that Melissa has gained a good deal of weight since the accident and that many of her peers could not physically catch her and keep her from hitting the floor. Mrs. Gust also brought up the subject of school liability. She noted that it was in the school district's best interests, as well as Melissa's, to use the best means of protection, and that, in the opinion of school health care professionals, was a helmet. Mrs. Zemke was already boiling at the idea of the helmet, but when Mrs. Gust mentioned Melissa's weight gain, she really got angry. She told Mrs. Gust that she was the most insensitive person that she had ever met, and that Melissa would never step foot in this school with a helmet on her head. She further stated that she did not know how Mrs. Gust became a middle school principal when it was obvious that she did not know anything about psychological development at this stage. Mr. Zemke tried to get his wife to calm down, but the discussion between the principal and Mrs. Zemke continued to escalate.

Mr. Zemke suggested another meeting to resolve these differences. They had yet to work out other issues that concerned the precipitation of Melissa's seizures. Many of the seizures appear to be triggered by visual stimulation. In Melissa's case, the flickering of fluorescent lights and visual patterns that have horizontal and vertical lines crossing, such as window panes and plaids, seem to be precipitants to seizure activity. The Zemkes had asked Mrs. Gust to request that all of Melissa's teachers avoid wearing plaids and to make sure that the blinds were pulled down in all of her classrooms so that she would not be exposed to the window pane configuration. Although Mrs. Gust did not turn down those requests, the Zemkes had the impression that she was resistant to making these modifications.

Background Information:

Prior to the bicycle accident, Melissa was a cheerleader and winner of the local Junior Miss competition, in which she chose dance as her area of talent. Since the accident, Melissa has not regained her gross or fine motor skills. She had to drop off the cheer-

© 2005 by PRO-ED, Inc. All rights reserved. Duplicating this page is strictly prohibited.

CASE STUDIES

leading squad, and she no longer dances. Her recuperation required a lengthy period of hospitalization in which she was bedridden. As a result of this inactivity, she has gained over 30 pounds. This weight gain has caused additional self-concept problems that Melissa is struggling to overcome. Her mother is particularly sensitive to comments about Melissa's new appearance because she knows it is a source of depression for Melissa. It is also a reminder to Mrs. Zemke that she has lost the daughter she had before the head injury.

Case Study Activity

Individual or Group Case Analysis

Answer the following questions and be prepared to discuss them in class.

1. Does the school have the legal right to make Melissa wear a helmet during the school day? Do the parents have the legal right to specify how Melissa's teachers should dress?

_____

_____

_____

_____

_____

_____

2. To what does the term *secondary brain damage* refer? Do you think that Melissa should wear a helmet to prevent secondary brain injury from falling as a result of a seizure, or do you think that students should be trained for seizure management? Do you have any other ideas for preventing secondary brain injury?

_____

_____

_____

_____

_____

_____

© 2005 by PRO-ED, Inc. All rights reserved. Duplicating this page is strictly prohibited.

3. What is a tonic-clonic seizure? What types of medication are typically used to control this type of seizure? Can these seizures be precipitated by the flickering of lights and certain visual patterns? If you were one of Melissa's teachers, how would you feel about dress modifications and keeping the blinds pulled down to assist this student?

_____

_____

_____

_____

_____

_____

_____

4. Was it insensitive of Mrs. Gust to mention Melissa's weight gain? Do you think that Mrs. Zemke overreacted or was her anger justified?

_____

_____

_____

_____

_____

_____

_____

5. What kinds of supports will Melissa need as she transitions into high school next year?

_____

_____

_____

_____

_____

_____

_____

© 2005 by PRO-ED, Inc. All rights reserved. Duplicating this page is strictly prohibited.

CASE STUDIES

6. Create A Question (optional)

_____

_____

_____

_____

_____

_____

_____

_____

Nicole

Nicole is a 5-year-old child who will be attending Hinckley Elementary School in a couple of months. For the past 2 years, Nicole has been in a special education preschool program. Nicole has cerebral palsy, which affects all four limbs to the extent that she requires a wheelchair for mobility. The pupil assessment team believes that she has severe mental retardation, but there is still some question about cognitive ability because she is nonverbal. The cerebral palsy has resulted in paralysis of the vocal folds. The assessment team feels that the extent of her cognitive disability will become more clear as Nicole develops.

Nicole's mother, Mrs. Buras, wants her to attend a general education kindergarten class in her own neighborhood. The school district would rather have Nicole spend another year in the special education preschool program, which is located at a school about 10 miles away. The special education director thinks that the most appropriate education for Nicole would include intensive physical, occupational, and speech–language therapies. This is the focus of the curriculum in the special education preschool setting. She has told Mrs. Buras that if Nicole is in the general kindergarten, she will not be able to achieve many of the objectives that the other children will be working toward because of her communication and physical limitations. In addition to this concern, the special education director has also told Mrs. Buras that there will be no paraprofessional in the kindergarten class this year because of funding problems. Therefore, Nicole will not, in all probability, get the attention she needs. The kindergarten teacher, Mrs. Pekarus, does not see how she will manage 24 kindergartners without a paraprofessional, particularly with the addition of a child with multiple disabilities. After numerous meetings, it was decided that Nicole would go to a general education kindergarten class, but only if Mrs. Buras could attend with her to help out. Mrs. Buras was elated about the decision. She really felt that this was the kind of environment that would stimulate Nicole's acquisition of new skills.

Three weeks into the kindergarten year, Mrs. Buras is starting to feel the strain of her new schedule. She is having a difficult time keeping up with her responsibilities to her three other children, as well as being with Nicole at school on a daily basis. When she brought this to Mrs. Pekarus's attention, the teacher remarked that everyone has to make difficult decisions. She was sure that Nicole would be just as happy in the special education program if Mrs. Buras decided that was what she had to do. Mrs. Buras had been hoping that Mrs. Pekarus would respond by

© 2005 by PRO-ED, Inc. All rights reserved. Duplicating this page is strictly prohibited.

Physical Disabilities and Health Impairments

saying that she did not need to be there every day or that she now realized that Nicole was not the burden she had anticipated. She felt very dejected when she realized that 3 weeks with Nicole in the classroom had done nothing to change this teacher's mind. It was obvious that Mrs. Pekarus still did not want Nicole in her classroom.

Background Information:

Mrs. Buras has felt as if she has been fighting the system ever since Nicole started in the preschool program. She knows that the special education personnel think that Nicole has severe or profound retardation, even though they readily admit that they do not have the appropriate tests to determine her potential. Mrs. Buras has the distinct impression that they have already decided that Nicole will never communicate, even though they talk a lot about the importance of clinical communication therapy. For a long time, she has wanted to get her daughter out of the clutches of this special education team to see how she would function in a group of her peers. Mrs. Buras feels that being around children who are verbal may be much more stimulating than being in a special education classroom where no one talks except the therapists.

The special education director, pupil assessment team, and Mrs. Pekarus believe that Mrs. Buras has not accepted the fact that Nicole has severe retardation. They have spent considerable time as a group talking about how to assist this mother in shifting from her current stage of denial into a more realistic state of acceptance of the disability. They feel that once Mrs. Buras has accepted the extent of the disability, she will be in a position to more rationally discuss the necessity of specialized services for Nicole.

 # Case Study Activity

Individual or Group Case Analysis

Answer the following questions and be prepared to discuss them in class.

1. Do you think Mrs. Buras is in a state of denial regarding her daughter's disability? Is it possible that the assessment team is wrong about Nicole's mental retardation? What factors would interfere with a valid assessment of her potential at this point in her development?

_____

_____

_____

_____

_____

_____

_____

_____

© 2005 by PRO-ED, Inc. All rights reserved. Duplicating this page is strictly prohibited.

2. What is your opinion regarding the most appropriate placement for Nicole? Provide support for your response. Why do you think the school district is so intent on having this child in a segregated setting?

_____

_____

_____

_____

_____

_____

_____

3. Can the school district actually require Mrs. Buras to assist her daughter as a contingency for school attendance? Are there any laws that would influence this situation?

_____

_____

_____

_____

_____

_____

_____

4. Is it possible that this child's needs could be accommodated in Mrs. Pekarus's classroom without the assistance of Mrs. Buras? If you were the kindergarten teacher, what would your position be with regard to having this child in your classroom?

_____

_____

_____

_____

_____

_____

_____

© 2005 by PRO-ED, Inc. All rights reserved. Duplicating this page is strictly prohibited.

5. Do you agree or disagree with Mrs. Buras's idea that communicative interaction with Nicole's peers might be more stimulating than the communication therapy delivered by special education personnel? What assistive devices might be implemented to encourage her communication ability?

_____

_____

_____

_____

_____

_____

6. Create A Question (optional)

_____

_____

_____

_____

_____

_____

_____

Robert

Robert is a 16-year-old sophomore at Blue Springs High School. He was diagnosed as having cerebral palsy shortly after he turned 1 year of age. Although his legs are the most severely affected, he also has restricted movement on the right side of his upper body. His limited body movement is characterized by spasticity, and his speech is characterized by dysarthria, which interferes with intelligibility. This is Robert's second year at Blue Springs High. Last year, his guidance counselor, Mr. Kelso, worked with Robert and his mother to carefully choose courses that would be appropriate for his interests and educational needs. Robert receives speech therapy three times per week, as well as the services of a physical therapist to assist him with mobility exercises. He does not require any academic assistance. His grades last year were all Bs and Cs. Mr. Kelso is responsible for coordinating Robert's IEP, which will include a transition plan this year.

Last year, Robert wanted to take French, but Mr. Kelso talked him out of it. He did not feel that Robert would be successful in that class because of

© 2005 by PRO-ED, Inc. All rights reserved. Duplicating this page is strictly prohibited.

CASE STUDIES

his speech problems. This year, Robert appears to be more determined to take French. His mother, Ms. Michaud, is supporting him. When Mr. Kelso went to talk with the French teacher, Mrs. Bourcier, he did not get a warm reception. She has seen Robert in the halls, so she is somewhat familiar with him. She told Mr. Kelso that it was absolutely out of the question for Robert to be in her class. When Ms. Michaud was told of the French teacher's position, she decided to talk to her in person. She approached Mrs. Bourcier in a very tactful manner, explaining to her that her son wanted to learn French more than any other subject, and she was sure he would do well in that class. Mrs. Bourcier told Ms. Michaud that it would not be possible to have "a student like that" in French class, and that "there are many other courses for students like your son." After many years of dealing with attitudes like Mrs. Bourcier's, Ms. Michaud has determined that the best way to respond to these situations is to calmly stand her ground, so she kept repeating, "Robert would really like to be in your class." Mrs. Bourcier continued to defend her position by saying, "Your son can't be in my class because I can't understand what he's saying in English. How could I evaluate him in French?" and "It wouldn't be fair to him, he'll flunk." Ms. Michaud ended the conference by saying that Robert would look forward to studying with her. Mrs. Bourcier decided to let Mr. Kelso deal with this matter.

Meanwhile, Mr. Kelso has been interviewing Robert with regard to his vocational interests so that a transition plan can be developed for him. Robert has told Mr. Kelso that he wants to be a commercial airline pilot, and he is not interested in learning any other skills in terms of a vocation. He has agreed to the community living skills program, which will include grocery shopping, checkbook balancing, and budgeting, but he does not want to be involved in any of the vocational programs. Robert wants to take all of the courses that are considered to be prerequisites for the college-bound student. Mr. Kelso does not think this is a good idea, as he is sure that Robert is going to have considerable problems with many of those classes. He is also not sure how he should counsel Robert with regard to his flying ambitions. Ms. Michaud has indicated to Mr. Kelso that Robert is going through a sensitive period. He is feeling left out because he is not getting his driver's license, dating, or participating in sports. She mentioned that she is also unsure of how to advise him on certain things because he has been "flying off the handle" a lot lately when she makes certain suggestions.

Another problem that has arisen for this student concerns Robert's use of a walker. Several of Robert's teachers have complained to Mr. Kelso that Robert is always late to class because it takes him so long to move from room to room. They feel that he would do better if he did not miss the first 10 minutes of class. Two of these teachers have also complained that it is distracting to the other students to have Robert come in late and take an additional 5 minutes to struggle over to his seat. Mr. Kelso mentioned this to Robert's physical therapist, Mrs. Cox. She told Mr. Kelso that she has been recommending for some time now that Robert give up the walker for a wheelchair, but he refuses to follow this suggestion. Mrs. Cox feels that it is a sensitive topic for Robert at this stage in his development, so she has not pressed the issue.

Mr. Kelso has now realized that there are three important issues that he needs to resolve for this student—enrolling in the French class, using the walker versus the wheelchair, and setting vocational goals. Because these issues involve the cooperation of different people, he is thinking that he should call a conference to discuss the situation. He likes Robert, and he hopes to help him work out some of these difficulties without hurting his feelings.

Background Information:

Robert's father was a Canadian Air Force pilot who married his mother when she was studying in Quebec. When Robert was diagnosed with cerebral palsy, the doctor painted a grim picture of all the things that Robert would never be able to do. This was apparently too much for his father to accept because he left the family shortly thereafter. Robert's mother stayed on in Quebec for a year after the divorce, hoping that Robert's father might show some interest in his son, but that was not to be the case. Robert's father never came back to visit his son after he had left. Ms. Michaud decided to return to the United States, where she would have the support of her family.

Although Robert's father has never contacted him, Robert is still very much aware of him. He keeps a framed picture of him on his bureau amidst the model airplanes that are part of his collection. He occasionally asks his mother for details about his father's life. Ms. Michaud has never hinted that his

© 2005 by PRO-ED, Inc. All rights reserved. Duplicating this page is strictly prohibited.

father could not accept Robert's disability, but she suspects that Robert understands the truth. Her greatest fear is that Robert will one day call him on the phone and that his father will hang up on him.

What Ms. Michaud does not realize is that Robert has already done this. Although Mr. Michaud did hang up on Robert, it was because he did not understand Robert's speech and thought it was a prank call.

Case Study Activities

Part I:
Role Playing

Break into groups of five students. Simulate a conference in which the three different issues facing this student are resolved. The following roles should be assumed: Robert, Mr. Kelso, Mrs. Cox, Ms. Michaud, and Mrs. Bourcier. Write a summary of the resolution, being sure to address each of the three issues.

Resolution

_____

_____

_____

_____

_____

_____

_____

_____

_____

_____

_____

_____

_____

_____

_____

© 2005 by PRO-ED, Inc. All rights reserved. Duplicating this page is strictly prohibited.

CASE STUDIES

Part II:
Individual or Group Case Analysis

Answer the following questions and be prepared to discuss them in class.

1. Do you think Mr. Kelso should counsel Robert out of the idea of becoming a commercial airline pilot? Does Robert's disability preclude him from meeting the requirements for this profession?

_____

_____

_____

_____

_____

_____

2. Does Mrs. Bourcier have the right to exclude Robert from her French class on the basis of his speech problem? What modifications could she use to encourage his success in this class? Are there assistive devices that would enhance Robert's success in this class?

_____

_____

_____

_____

_____

_____

3. Should Robert use a wheelchair instead of a walker? Why do you think he is resistant to the idea of giving up his walker? If he continues to use the walker, how can the problem of tardiness be alleviated?

_____

_____

_____

_____

_____

_____

© 2005 by PRO-ED, Inc. All rights reserved. Duplicating this page is strictly prohibited.

4. Do you think Robert's adolescent development has anything to do with his recent reactions to suggestions from his mother, guidance counselor, and teachers? Are there any other factors in Robert's life that may be causing him to experience stress?

_____

_____

_____

_____

_____

_____

_____

5. Is Robert at risk for developing depression? How can teachers and counselors support a student whose disability imposes significant restrictions on development?

_____

_____

_____

_____

_____

_____

_____

6. Create A Question (optional)

_____

_____

_____

_____

_____

_____

© 2005 by PRO-ED, Inc. All rights reserved. Duplicating this page is strictly prohibited.

Travis

Travis is a 4-year-old preschool student at Clarkson Elementary School. He had been adjusting well in his preschool program, but his teacher, Mrs. Ellsworth, started to notice that he was experiencing respiratory problems. These respiratory problems seemed to be associated with the cold viruses that continually make their way around the preschool class. Whenever Travis got a cold, Mrs. Ellsworth observed that he appeared to have difficulty breathing and experienced significant coughing episodes. The preschool teacher called Travis's mother, Ms. Shoemacher, to have him picked up on several occasions because his breathing was so labored.

Last month, Travis ended up in the hospital on oxygen because of a particularly severe upper respiratory virus that caused major breathing problems. When he came back to school, Ms. Shoemacher brought a nebulizer and medication to be administered during the school day. Mrs. Ellsworth was caught off guard when she saw all the medical supplies—face mask, solution cup, saline solution to be measured and mixed with a prescription drug, and tubing for the machine. When Ms. Shoemacher started explaining the measurement, administration, and cleaning of equipment, Mrs. Ellsworth stopped her, saying, "Ms. Shoemacher, I am not a doctor or a nurse. I simply could not take the responsibility for giving this medical treatment to your son." Ms. Shoemacher seemed surprised and hurt by Mrs. Ellsworth's reaction. She told her that if she did not agree to help with the treatment that Travis would not be able to come to school. Mrs. Ellsworth apologized, but said that even though she had a paraprofessional, there was no way they had the time to stop the preschool activities for 16 children to provide this treatment for Travis. Ms. Shoemacher gathered up Travis and his equipment and quietly left the room without saying anything else. Mrs. Ellsworth could see that tears were running down her face. Travis was confused and upset. Mrs. Ellsworth felt terrible. But what else could she do?

Background Information:

Travis's preschool is a public school program admin-istered by the South County School District. The parents of the preschoolers pay the tuition that provides the preschool teachers' salaries, whereas the school district provides the space and the materials for the program. It is an extended-day preschool with hours from 8 A.M. to 3 P.M.

Travis was diagnosed as having asthma at the age of 3. His mother has worked hard to minimize this condition so that Travis could have a normal childhood. Travis always had a nanny before he went to preschool, so she was able to provide him with the nebulizer treatments he needed. Last year, Travis's father and mother were divorced and, since that time, Ms. Shoemacher has struggled financially. Mr. Shoemacher has paid sporadic child support, and he sees Travis about every other month. Travis and Ms. Shoemacher had to leave their home and move into an apartment when the bank foreclosed on the mortgage. Ms. Shoemacher also had to let the nanny go because she could no longer afford her. She put Travis in a home day-care situation, which lasted for about 6 months. The day-care provider started getting nervous about Travis's breathing. She finally told Ms. Shoemacher that she was getting too old to take on this kind of responsibility, and she could no longer care for Travis.

Ms. Shoemacher felt as if she was at the end of her rope when she heard about the public preschool program in her school district. She arranged to have her work hours run from 8:30 to 2:30, with the provision that she take work home every evening to make up for the other 2 hours of the 8-hour work day. She was just starting to hope that things might work out for Travis and her. The emotional turmoil and stress caused by the recent events of the divorce, the change in living arrangements, and the effort to cover the hospital bills for Travis were starting to overwhelm her. She decided not to say anything to the preschool about Travis's condition, hoping that if she gave him a treatment in the morning, he would be able to make it through the rest of the day until she could pick him up in the afternoon and give him another treatment.

© 2005 by PRO-ED, Inc. All rights reserved. Duplicating this page is strictly prohibited.

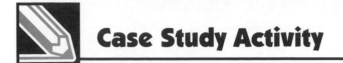

Case Study Activity

Individual or Group Case Analysis

Answer the following questions and be prepared to discuss them in class.

1. Should Ms. Shoemacher have told the school about Travis's asthma? Why or why not?

_____

_____

_____

_____

_____

_____

_____

_____

_____

2. Is it unreasonable to expect Mrs. Ellsworth or her paraprofessional to provide Travis with this treatment during school hours? Do public schools typically provide this type of service?

_____

_____

_____

_____

_____

_____

_____

_____

_____

© 2005 by PRO-ED, Inc. All rights reserved. Duplicating this page is strictly prohibited.

CASE STUDIES

3. Does the school have a legal right to refuse to enroll Travis because of his medical condition? What laws could influence this situation? How far should schools be expected to go in terms of providing different treatments to meet the needs of children?

_____

_____

_____

_____

_____

_____

_____

_____

4. What kind of preschool should Travis be in? Should Ms. Shoemacher be looking into schools that are associated with hospitals, or should she be pursuing placement in the general education public school classroom?

_____

_____

_____

_____

_____

_____

_____

_____

5. It is obvious that Mrs. Ellsworth is an empathic teacher who is struggling with this problem. If you were this teacher, what would you do to resolve this situation?

_____

_____

_____

_____

_____

_____

_____

© 2005 by PRO-ED, Inc. All rights reserved. Duplicating this page is strictly prohibited.

6. Create A Question (optional)

_____

_____

_____

_____

_____

_____

_____

© 2005 by PRO-ED, Inc. All rights reserved. Duplicating this page is strictly prohibited.

CHAPTER 6

Communication Disorders

Kayla

Kayla is a 4-year-old child at Cedar Point Elementary School. She is a student in Mrs. Chung's kindergarten classroom of 24 students. Kayla is a very bright little girl whose IQ falls in the gifted range. Although she will not turn 5 for another month, she is reading on the second-grade level. Her math skills are considered to be somewhat lower, at approximately the mid–first-grade level. Kayla has a severe speech impairment that significantly interferes with her communication. Her vocalizations are basically unintelligible to all except her family. When Kayla tries to speak, she is not able to articulate sounds in a typical fashion. Her speech is similar to that of a profoundly deaf individual who is not able to reproduce speech sounds.

Mrs. Chung understands very little of anything that Kayla says. The other kindergartners are also unable to comprehend her speech. This has created a very frustrating learning environment for this child, so that she resorts to temper tantrums when she cannot make her needs known. Kayla will pick up any nearby object—such as a book, pencil holder, globe, or chair—and hurl it as far as she can without regard for those who may be in the path of these objects. Kayla has been in Mrs. Chung's classroom for 3 weeks and, during this brief time, her mother has been called to the school more than eight times to pick her up because of behavioral incidents. Mrs. Chung is very anxious about this situation. She is afraid that a student will be injured during one of Kayla's temper tantrums.

Kayla has speech therapy for 20 minutes per day with Ms. Gordon, the speech therapist. Mrs. Chung is grateful for this therapy because for 20 minutes Kayla will be out of the room, and she will be free to teach her students without fear of objects flying around the room. When Mrs. Chung told Ms. Gordon that she was having a difficult time with Kayla's behavior, she seemed understanding and gave her a book of behavior management strategies. Unfortunately, Mrs. Chung has not had the opportunity to try any of these because Kayla ends up being sent home so frequently. She feels as if she is not making any progress whatsoever. Mrs. Chung is hesitant to go to the principal because she thinks he might think that she cannot manage her own class. This is Mrs. Chung's first year in the classroom, and she is starting to think that she should quit teaching and go to work for her father's travel agency.

Background Information:

Kayla's birth was a very difficult one. She was lodged in the birth canal for a long period of time before the obstetrician decided on a cesarean delivery. At the time of her birth, her Apgar was 5 at one minute and 6 at five minutes. Her pediatrician was very concerned about possible trauma from the birth. However, as Kayla began to demonstrate normal achievement of developmental milestones, such as rolling over, crawling, and walking, he became less concerned. Although her speech milestones did not seem to be coming along as well as her development in other areas, the pediatrician told her parents, Mr. and Mrs. McKenzie, not to worry because Kayla's receptive language was well above average. He assumed that expressive language would follow on its own schedule of development. This assurance seemed to satisfy Mr. McKenzie, but not Mrs. McKenzie, who wanted to take Kayla to a specialist for an independent evaluation. Mr. McKenzie refused to have this done and accused Mrs. McKenzie of being neurotic, among other things. The couple fought bitterly over this point for a year and a half. During this time, Kayla's behavior became worse and worse. Because she could not make her needs known to her parents, she became so frustrated that she would release her anger by throwing any nearby objects. Things eventually became so bad that, little by little, all breakables were put away so that Kayla would not throw them in a fit of anger. The family substituted plastic dishes for their stoneware and plastic tumblers for their glassware. Babysitters would come only once—the first time— and were never available thereafter. Although Mr. and Mrs. McKenzie did not acknowledge it, their home often resembled a war zone.

Finally, Mrs. McKenzie took Kayla to a child development clinic when she turned 4. She was diagnosed as having a severe speech impairment, and it was recommended that she begin therapy immediately. When Mr. McKenzie found out Mrs. McKenzie

© 2005 by PRO-ED, Inc. All rights reserved. Duplicating this page is strictly prohibited.

CASE STUDIES

had taken his daughter for an evaluation in spite of his objection, he moved out of the family home. Kayla's behavior seemed to become even worse after this. Mrs. McKenzie's anxiety increased, and she began to have bouts of depression that depleted her energy. When her husband was in the house, she was able to try to manage Kayla's behavior, but with Mr. McKenzie gone, it was as if she just gave up. She knows that she is about to lose her job because of Kayla's problems at school, but she feels helpless to do anything about it.

 ## Case Study Activity

Individual or Group Case Analysis

Answer the following questions and be prepared to discuss them in class.

1. Whom should Mrs. Chung go to for help? Should she explain her situation to the principal? Should the speech therapist be giving her additional help?

_____

_____

_____

_____

_____

_____

_____

2. What is the relationship between Kayla's behavior and her speech impairment? Is sending Kayla home for throwing things a good strategy for managing this behavior? What other strategies might Mrs. Chung try?

_____

_____

_____

_____

_____

_____

_____

© 2005 by PRO-ED, Inc. All rights reserved. Duplicating this page is strictly prohibited.

3. How could assistive technology be implemented to assist Kayla in her communication?

_____

_____

_____

_____

_____

_____

_____

4. Does Kayla represent a danger to the other students in the classroom? Should she be in the general education classroom? Why or why not?

_____

_____

_____

_____

_____

_____

_____

_____

5. What has Kayla learned about misbehavior from her home environment? Has this influenced her behavior at school? Would a home-school behavior management plan be helpful to this family? How could such a plan be developed and implemented?

_____

_____

_____

_____

_____

_____

_____

© 2005 by PRO-ED, Inc. All rights reserved. Duplicating this page is strictly prohibited.

CASE STUDIES

6. Create A Question (optional)

_____

_____

_____

_____

_____

_____

_____

Mark

Mark is a 12-year-old sixth grader at Rushing East Middle School. Mrs. Clark, his English teacher, and Mrs. Orvieta, his Spanish teacher, have expressed concerns that he seems to be extremely reticent and socially withdrawn in class. Mrs. Orvieta is especially concerned because so much of Mark's grade is dependent upon his class participation. Mark is never late for class and always scores high on the written Spanish exams, yet he just sits and shakes his head when she asks him to respond to her questions in Spanish. Mrs. Clark's concerns are somewhat similar. Mark's written work is excellent, but he refuses to answer questions in class. She reads his papers and feels that he is one of her best students, but he does not seem to know the answers to any questions she asks in class. She is starting to wonder if maybe his parents might be writing his papers for him. Both teachers have shared their thoughts with Mr. Exner, the school counselor.

When Mr. Exner interviewed Mark, he had the same thoughts that his teachers shared. Mark impressed him as an adolescent who did not have much to say and was not too concerned about his academic progress. The only rise Mr. Exner got out of him was when he suggested that Mark might drop Spanish and substitute a class that required less participation. Mark shook his head vehemently and said, "No." When Mr. Exner reviewed Mark's cumulative folder, he discovered that Mark had received services for speech from kindergarten through the fifth grade. Mr. Exner decided to request Mark's special education file. When this file arrived, he found that Mark had been diagnosed with a severe fluency disorder in kindergarten and had received speech therapy for this problem until the fifth grade. At that time, the parents requested that the therapy be discontinued when Mark went on to middle school.

Background Information:

Mark's parents, Mr. and Mrs. Lupek, did not want speech therapy to be discontinued. Their son begged them to discontinue the service because he felt it would be too stigmatizing in middle school to be pulled out of class to work with the speech therapist. Mark also felt that he had made little progress with his stuttering in all those years of therapy. Mr. and Mrs. Lupek reluctantly agreed. Mark basically convinced them that he had gone as far as he could in speech therapy and "the rest is up to me." He also convinced them that his time was better spent in content

© 2005 by PRO-ED, Inc. All rights reserved. Duplicating this page is strictly prohibited.

areas and that he knew all the therapy strategies and could practice at home. Because Mark is a very bright and mature adolescent, the Lupeks decided to let him make the decision regarding speech therapy in middle school.

As it turns out, Mark's only compensatory strategy for his fluency disorder has been to stop talking. He feels that in middle school he can "make it" with his written work, and he will probably do better socially if he talks less.

Case Study Activity

Individual or Group Case Analysis

Answer the following questions and be prepared to discuss them in class.

1. Should Mark be in speech therapy in middle school? Is it likely that Mark will eventually grow out of his stuttering problem without continued therapy?

_____

_____

_____

_____

_____

_____

_____

2. Do you agree with the Lupeks' decision to let Mark decide what is best for himself because he is a "very bright and mature adolescent?" Why or why not?

_____

_____

_____

_____

_____

_____

_____

© 2005 by PRO-ED, Inc. All rights reserved. Duplicating this page is strictly prohibited.

3. Why do you think Mark did not mind speech therapy in elementary school, but now refuses this service in middle school? Give three reasons.

_____

_____

_____

_____

_____

_____

_____

4. What can teachers do in the classroom to decrease the stress that stutterers feel when speaking and to discourage others from teasing the speaker? Give four strategies.

_____

_____

_____

_____

_____

_____

_____

5. Should Mark drop out of Spanish because of its oral participation requirement? What modifications could be implemented to enhance his success in this class?

_____

_____

_____

_____

_____

_____

_____

© 2005 by PRO-ED, Inc. All rights reserved. Duplicating this page is strictly prohibited.

6. Create A Question (optional)

_____

_____

_____

_____

_____

_____

_____

_____

Richard

Richard is a 9-year-old student at Canyon Hills Elementary. He has recently moved to this town in Montana from Louisiana. Mr. Osage, Richard's third-grade teacher, has referred Richard for special education evaluation because of a speech problem. Mr. Osage estimates that anywhere from 50% to 75% of Richard's speech is unintelligible. Richard has been in the third grade for a month now, and things seem to be getting worse for this child. He does not appear to have any friends, and Mr. Osage attributes this to Richard's speech problem—his classmates cannot understand him either. Mr. Osage is disturbed that his third graders are making fun of Richard's speech. He has noticed that Richard is becoming more and more withdrawn, but he is not sure what to do about it. Mr. Osage has called the parents, Mr. and Mrs. Arceneau, in to discuss Richard's problem, only to discover that they have the same speech pattern as their son. Mr. Osage believes now that the problem must be of a genetic nature. He hopes that the pupil assessment team can identify Richard's problem, so that he can be placed in a class where he will receive the help he apparently needs. Mr. and Mrs. Arceneau seemed upset about the special education evaluation, saying that their son has not had school problems in the past.

Background Information:

Richard's cumulative folder from Louisiana indicates that he received all As and Bs on previous report cards. Teachers wrote only positive remarks about his behavior and academic progress. Mr. Osage is puzzled by the fact that he seems to be doing so poorly in his new school. He wonders if Richard is developing an emotional problem that is interfering with his school achievement. The speech therapist, Mrs. Gerkin, who has been practicing for 30 years, told Mr. Osage that she has never heard a speech pattern similar to that of Richard's. However, Mrs. Gerkin was born and raised in Montana, and she prides herself in telling others that there is no reason to leave the state because it is the most beautiful in the country. She is looking forward to completing her evaluation of Richard because she has never had a case such as this. She will probably recommend that Richard be staffed into a special education language delay class in a neighboring school district 25 miles away.

© 2005 by PRO-ED, Inc. All rights reserved. Duplicating this page is strictly prohibited.

CASE STUDIES

Case Study Activity

Individual or Group Case Analysis

Answer the following questions and be prepared to discuss them in class.

1. What do you think of Mr. Osage's observation that Richard's speech problem is genetic because his parents share the same pattern of speech? Is there another explanation?

_____

_____

_____

_____

_____

_____

2. Why would Mrs. Gerkin want Richard to be staffed into a language delay class when his Louisiana reports indicate his achievement is normal? Do you think this is an appropriate placement for Richard?

_____

_____

_____

_____

_____

_____

3. Mr. Osage's position seems to be that it is normal for his third graders to make fun of Richard, and that there is nothing he can do about it. If you were this teacher, describe three specific strategies you would use to socially integrate this student into your classroom.

_____

_____

_____

_____

_____

_____

© 2005 by PRO-ED, Inc. All rights reserved. Duplicating this page is strictly prohibited.

4. What types of assistive technology could be used to support this student's learning and socialization at Canyon Hills? Would these supports need to be temporary or long term?

_____

_____

_____

_____

_____

_____

_____

5. Explain the distinction between language disorders and language differences. Should speech–language therapy be provided regardless of whether the variation is sociocultural or pathological in nature? Why or why not?

_____

_____

_____

_____

_____

_____

_____

6. Create A Question (optional)

_____

_____

_____

_____

_____

_____

_____

© 2005 by PRO-ED, Inc. All rights reserved. Duplicating this page is strictly prohibited.

CASE STUDIES

Yuri

Yuri is a 16-year-old student at Woodrow Wilson High School. Yuri and his family immigrated to the United States from Azerbaijan 2 years ago. Yuri was recently evaluated by the pupil assessment team. His IQ testing suggested that he was functioning in the mildly retarded range, with adaptive behavior skills falling in the borderline to below normal range. The pupil assessment team at Woodrow Wilson has recommended that Yuri be identified as mentally retarded so he can receive special education services in his general education classes. Woodrow Wilson does not have any pull-out programs. The philosophy of the school is to provide additional help in the classroom to assist the student with the general education objectives.

Yuri's parents do not speak English, but his uncle, who does, has come to the school meetings to listen to the recommendations and interpret them to Yuri's parents, Mr. and Mrs. Scrincosky. The family is adamantly opposed to the idea of having their son identified as having mental retardation, but they recognize the fact that he needs help. The assessment team has told the family that Yuri does not qualify for special services under any other disability, so if he is going to get help, the parents will have to sign the papers that specify mental retardation as the disability condition.

Background Information:

When Yuri entered Woodrow Wilson 2 years ago, he did not speak any English. He was placed in the English as a Second Language (ESL) program. His ESL teacher, Mrs. Cuvo, was an energetic teacher who was firmly committed to the collaborative model of service delivery. She developed a program for Yuri that was based on close cooperation with his general education teachers. Mrs. Cuvo kept a detailed notebook of Yuri's curriculum and assignments for each class so that she could assist him with the achievement of specific goals for each subject. Although Yuri's grades fell into the C to D range, Mrs. Cuvo felt that he was making significant progress, considering his lack of familiarity with the English language.

After 2 years of receiving these educational services, Yuri took the conversational proficiency exam, which the district requires of all students. He passed the test and was immediately staffed out of the ESL program. Mrs. Cuvo did not want Yuri to leave the program, but it is the school district's policy to staff out all students who reach conversational proficiency on the ESL exam. Without Mrs. Cuvo's assistance, Yuri promptly began flunking all of his subjects. At this point, his general education teachers, wanting to help him, referred him for special education evaluation.

Although the members of the assessment team are well aware of Yuri's language difficulties, they believe that his school problems are related to his limited potential as opposed to his lack of proficiency in English. This position is based on the premise that because Yuri has passed the ESL exam, he has achieved proficiency in the language. The speech–language therapist on the pupil assessment team is the only member who is not in agreement with this recommendation. However, she has decided to go along with the team's recommendation because she knows Yuri needs help, and this is the only way he is going to receive it. She does not think that the stigma associated with the label of "mental retardation" should be considered an obstacle to getting services for this adolescent.

© 2005 by PRO-ED, Inc. All rights reserved. Duplicating this page is strictly prohibited.

Case Study Activity

Individual or Group Case Analysis

Answer the following questions and be prepared to discuss them in class.

1. Does the diagnosis of mental retardation appear to be appropriate in Yuri's case? Why or why not?

_____

_____

_____

_____

_____

_____

2. What do adaptive behavior scales measure? What kinds of items might appear on these tests? Why do you think Yuri's scores were so low on this test?

_____

_____

_____

_____

_____

_____

3. What is the purpose of a conversational proficiency exam? What is the relationship between conversational proficiency and academic achievement? Would it be possible to pass such an exam and still not have the language skills necessary for academic achievement?

_____

_____

_____

_____

_____

_____

© 2005 by PRO-ED, Inc. All rights reserved. Duplicating this page is strictly prohibited.

CASE STUDIES

4. What do you think Mr. and Mrs. Scrincosky should do? Should they accept the special education services even though they do not agree with the label of mental retardation? What would you recommend in this situation?

_____

_____

_____

_____

_____

_____

_____

_____

5. What type of educational plan would be the most appropriate for Yuri's instructional needs? How could assistive technology be used to support this student's access to the curriculum?

_____

_____

_____

_____

_____

_____

_____

_____

6. Create A Question (optional)

_____

_____

_____

_____

_____

_____

_____

_____

© 2005 by PRO-ED, Inc. All rights reserved. Duplicating this page is strictly prohibited.

CHAPTER 7

Autistic Spectrum Disorders

Brenna

Brenna is a 6-year-old first-grade student at Westfall Elementary School. From the age of 3, she has been in a special education program for preschool students with disabilities. This is Brenna's first year in the mainstream. Her first-grade teacher, Mrs. Escamilla, volunteered to have Brenna in her classroom, but she is starting to have second thoughts. Brenna's behavior has been quite disruptive to Mrs. Escamilla's class. When Brenna becomes upset, she makes loud guttural sounds for long periods of time and beats her fist on the desk. Sometimes, when she is very upset, she falls to the floor and rolls around while making the loud noises. These incidents last anywhere from 30 to 45 minutes and appear to be precipitated by noises in the classroom environment. For example, the pencil sharpener always causes a problem. A siren down the street, children walking by the classroom, a film being shown to a neighboring class, or any announcement over the public address system can potentially cause Brenna to experience stress. Although Brenna has a full-time paraprofessional assigned to her, this person is not able to calm her enough to stop the outbursts.

Mrs. Escamilla believes in inclusion, but she is starting to question whether this is the most suitable learning environment for Brenna. She is also concerned about her other students. She can tell they are frustrated by their classroom situation. Whenever Brenna has an outburst, the class has to stop all oral activities because of the noise level of the outburst. Mrs. Escamilla has gently broached the subject of placing Brenna into a special education classroom with Brenna's mother, Mrs. Lohrman, but she has had little success. Mrs. Lohrman felt that the 3 years Brenna spent in a preschool special education program were more negative than positive because of the behaviors exhibited by her classmates. Mrs. Escamilla does not know what to do now.

Background Information:

Mrs. Lohrman brought Brenna, at the age of 2, to the local university's developmental disabilities clinic for a complete evaluation. At that time, Brenna had little expressive language, numerous behavioral peculiarities, and limited social skills. The evaluation team felt that although Brenna displayed many autistic-like behaviors, such as self-stimulation, insistence on sameness, and poor interaction with the environment, she also displayed a pattern of high functioning on adaptive behavior measures and tests of visual–motor problem solving. They finally diagnosed her as being severely language impaired and recommended the special education preschool program for her. Mrs. Lohrman was hopeful that this program would give Brenna the communication and socialization skills necessary to begin first grade in a mainstream classroom. However, this program did not turn out to be ideal.

The preschool special education class served a population of children with multiple disabilities, and Brenna did not get the peer interaction that Mrs. Lohrman was hoping she would. Three of Brenna's classmates had autism; three had severe mental retardation and cerebral palsy; two were deaf and blind; and one child was nonverbal, nonambulatory, and profoundly retarded. In short, there was very little language stimulation in that classroom other than what was being provided by the specialists. Brenna's communication skills improved only slightly and, according to Mrs. Lohrman's perception, her behavior worsened. When she entered the program, her behaviors were mainly hand flapping and spinning. By the time she was staffed out of the program, she had added finger flicking and head slapping, much to her mother's dismay. After considerable thought, Mrs. Lohrman decided that Brenna would never again be subjected to a situation in which she would regress due to the atypical behavior exhibited by other children. She has experienced a lot of guilt for allowing her daughter to stay in that classroom for 3 years.

© 2005 by PRO-ED, Inc. All rights reserved. Duplicating this page is strictly prohibited.

CASE STUDIES

Case Study Activity

Individual or Group Case Analysis

Answer the following questions and be prepared to discuss them in class.

1. What kinds of interventions and resources could Mrs. Escamilla try to decrease Brenna's behavioral outbursts? Give four examples.

_____

_____

_____

_____

_____

2. Was Brenna's special education preschool class appropriate for her needs? Did it prepare her to make the transition to first grade?

_____

_____

_____

_____

_____

3. If you were the parent of one of Brenna's classmates in Mrs. Escamilla's class, would you take any action in this situation? Should disruptive children such as Brenna be excluded from mainstream classrooms?

_____

_____

_____

_____

_____

© 2005 by PRO-ED, Inc. All rights reserved. Duplicating this page is strictly prohibited.

4. Is it possible that Brenna's behavior problems are related to her severe language delay? How might these be related? How could assistive technology be used to increase her communication skills?

_____

_____

_____

_____

_____

_____

_____

_____

5. If you were Brenna's teacher, explain how you might work with her parent to increase this child's opportunity for success in the first grade.

_____

_____

_____

_____

_____

_____

_____

_____

6. Create A Question (optional)

_____

_____

_____

_____

_____

_____

_____

© 2005 by PRO-ED, Inc. All rights reserved. Duplicating this page is strictly prohibited.

CASE STUDIES

Greg

Greg is a 13-year-old seventh grader at Medford Middle School. He is currently failing three subjects and receiving Cs in the others. His mother, Mrs. Wiecinsky, is desperately trying to get him some help, but so far her requests have not been well received by Greg's teachers. Greg has been identified as having Asperger's syndrome by a psychiatrist in an independent evaluation. The psychiatrist's report stated that Greg would require some significant modifications in the school environment to help him achieve commensurate with his ability level. One of these modifications was that Greg's teachers should provide support for his role in group projects. Many of his classes in middle school require group projects that are worth a substantial number of points. Because of social problems, Greg has been unable to contribute to the group effort and loses all points for these assignments. His fellow group members also complain to the teacher that he refuses to participate when, in actuality, Greg is too anxious to assume the responsibilities of his role. This anxiety also interferes with his ability to follow what is going on in class; he believes that his classmates are staring at him, so he keeps his head down and focuses his attention on his mechanical pencil, the illustration on his book, or the lines on his notebook paper. Thus, he is frequently unaware of the teacher's instruction and the assignments given. Greg's psychiatrist has recommended that his teachers check with him at the end of class to see that he has written down the homework assignment and understands what he is to do. Another recommended modification specified that each teacher should ask him if he needs help when he is completing seatwork or taking an exam in class because Greg is unable to initiate the request for assistance. Mrs. Wiecinsky has not been able to convince a single teacher that Greg genuinely needs this assistance to be successful. Of the three courses that Greg is currently failing—social studies, English, and Spanish—none of the teachers is willing to make any changes whatsoever. These teachers seem to think that Greg is lazy and slow. Since Greg has not been identified as a student with special education needs, the teachers have taken the position that he should conform to the same expectations they hold for the rest of the class. One of these teachers has

also told Mrs. Wiecinsky that she does not believe there is such a thing as Asperger's syndrome, and that it sounds like an excuse for her son's failure to conform to school requirements.

When Mrs. Wiecinsky went to the principal to ask for help, he referred her to his assistant principal, who referred her to the guidance counselor, who gave her a list of local mental health professionals who might be able to counsel her son. Mrs. Wiecinsky feels as if she is at the end of her rope. She fears Greg will end up failing most of his subjects as he did last year. She does not know where to go or to whom to turn.

Background Information:

Greg has always been an unusual child in that he displayed a number of strengths in marked contrast to his weaknesses. For example, at the age of 6, he had memorized all the commuter train stops for the city of Chicago from a Chicago Transit Authority map that his aunt had inadvertently left at his home after taking a business trip to that city. Greg had never been to Chicago, nor was the family planning a trip to that destination. The city is 2,000 miles from his hometown, and he does not know anyone who lives there. In spite of the fact that this city did not seem to have any connection with his life, Greg began to display a great degree of enthusiasm in learning and reciting this information. Whenever Greg's mother would have company, Greg would immediately launch into a description of the different train lines, the specific stops, and the time between each stop. His extraordinary ability to memorize this information stood in marked contrast to his inability to memorize and use the simplest of polite conventions. He could never remember to say "hello" or "good-bye" to visitors. He never said "thank you" to anyone bringing him gifts. When his mother chided him about this, he always said, "I forget what to say." As far back as Mrs. Wiecinsky could remember, Greg has never had a friend. He has never been asked over to a child's home, with the exception of a couple of birthday parties to which his whole class had been invited.

Greg was able to be a fairly successful student throughout elementary school. His strengths in single word reading, math computations, and spelling (he

© 2005 by PRO-ED, Inc. All rights reserved. Duplicating this page is strictly prohibited.

won the school spelling bee every year for 6 years) were so great that teachers often overlooked his weaknesses in comprehension and problem solving. All of his teachers found him to be an unusual child because of his poor social skills and his continued interest in the Chicago Transit Authority commuter train lines.

When he started middle school, Greg immediately began having major school problems. His ability to answer true–false, fill-in-the-blank, and multiple-choice questions in elementary school did not prepare him for the essay question exams and expository assignments characteristic of the middle school curriculum. Many of his middle school subjects also require intensive group project collaborations, in which he is unable to participate because of his social impairment. At the end of the first reporting period, he was failing all subjects with the exception of math and science. His teachers identified the problem as a lack of motivation. Mrs. Wiecinsky initiated a parent referral and requested a full special education evaluation. Although the school did not think that this was necessary, they agreed to do the evaluation because Mrs. Wiecinsky demanded it. The results indicated that Greg's IQ was 95. Single-word reading was at the 10th-grade level, math computations were at the 9th-grade level, and spelling was above the 12th-grade level; however, math reasoning was found to be at the 4th-grade level and reading comprehension was at the 5th-grade level. Although the assessment team found his evaluation profile to be rather unusual, they did not find evidence of any specific learning problem that met the criteria for a disability condition. School officials told Mrs. Wiecinsky that Greg's social problems were unrelated to his school progress. They inferred that Greg's lack of motivation could be attributed to his parents' divorce 10 years prior and recommended that she get him a counselor to help him deal with this problem.

Case Study Activity

Individual or Group Case Analysis

Answer the following questions and be prepared to discuss them in class.

1. Explain the specific characteristics of Asperger's syndrome in relation to Greg's behavior and functioning. To what extent is this disability remediable?

_____

_____

_____

_____

_____

_____

_____

_____

© 2005 by PRO-ED, Inc. All rights reserved. Duplicating this page is strictly prohibited.

CASE STUDIES

2. Explain how it is possible for the psychiatrist's report to specify a disability condition, and yet the special education evaluation at the school did not uncover one. Why do you think Greg's teachers are refusing to provide him the assistance recommended in the psychiatrist's report?

_____

_____

_____

_____

_____

_____

_____

3. Does Mrs. Wiecinsky have any legal recourse if Greg's teachers continue to refuse to provide him with these modifications? Explain the different options that might be available to her.

_____

_____

_____

_____

_____

_____

_____

4. What type of transition supports will Greg need when he makes the transition from middle school to high school?

_____

_____

_____

_____

_____

_____

© 2005 by PRO-ED, Inc. All rights reserved. Duplicating this page is strictly prohibited.

5. If you were asked to be an advocate for this family, explain how you would help resolve this problem.

_____

_____

_____

_____

_____

_____

6. Create A Question (optional)

_____

_____

_____

_____

_____

_____

_____

Paul

Paul is a 16-year-old student at Middleton High School. He attends a program for adolescents with severe disabilities for most of the instructional day. He is mainstreamed for physical education and lunch. Paul is an autistic student with severe communication and socialization problems. Although he is verbal, the only way he can use language is to echo back what he has heard in his environment. He apparently has no formulation ability of his own. Facilitated communication has been tried with Paul, but without success. He has been successful in learning approximately six signs, and he has a language board with pictures of 10 events or requests that he sometimes uses.

Paul's social problems are of concern to both his teachers and his mother, Mrs. Wender. When Paul becomes frustrated, he physically strikes out at those in his environment. Sometimes he resorts to biting instead of hitting. Paul's special education teacher, Mr. Hirsch, believes that Paul is using physical aggression because of his frustration with communication. Many times he becomes so frustrated and upset that he forgets to use the communication system to which he has access. This has been a long-standing problem with Paul, but it has worsened as his size has increased. When he was young and small, his teachers and mother could more easily handle his outbursts. Now

© 2005 by PRO-ED, Inc. All rights reserved. Duplicating this page is strictly prohibited.

CASE STUDIES

that he is almost 5'10" and 200 pounds, his behavior has become more difficult to manage. Paul has a full-time paraprofessional, Mr. Jackson, whose sole responsibility is to assist Paul with his communication and socialization. Often, this means that Mr. Jackson has to physically restrain him from hitting another student in the classroom, in the physical education class, or in the hall.

In the classroom, Paul becomes easily upset if another student changes something in the environment, such as pulling the blinds down, moving a table around the room, or listening to an audiotape without using the headphones. Paul is very sensitive to these changes and appears to need a great deal of structure and sameness in his environment. Mr. Hirsch and Mr. Jackson have decided that the best way to work with Paul is to have a corner of the classroom designated as his space. They have structured the classroom in a way that provides Paul with an eight-by-eight-foot section that is surrounded by three-foot bookshelves on two sides and two adjoining walls on the other two sides. Mr. Jackson stays with Paul in this section and provides him one-to-one communication instruction. When Paul is having a good day, Mr. Jackson brings him out to interact with the other students in the classroom for as long as Paul can tolerate the interaction.

Although neither Mr. Hirsch nor Mr. Jackson would describe this program as being optimal, they both felt it was working pretty well considering the circumstances of Paul's behavior. Unfortunately, two incidents occurred that are causing them to rethink Paul's placement. During swimming, Paul attacked another student who dove in the pool in front of him in an attempt to swim over to his own class. It was clear that the student scared Paul, who reacted by grabbing his arm and refusing to let go. It took Mr. Jackson and two other teachers to pry Paul's hands off the student. Needless to say, the other student was pretty shaken up. Then, at lunch, another student came up behind Paul and gave him a pat on the back, taking Paul by surprise. Paul reacted by throwing his whole tray at the student and, again, he had to be restrained by several adults. The student who had greeted Paul was angry and embarrassed.

As a result of these attacks, the principal, Mrs. Yates, now has two complaints from angry parents. She has asked the pupil assessment team to review Paul's placement. Her feeling is that he needs to be in a more restrictive placement, such as a special school that serves students with severe behavioral needs. Mrs. Wender is upset because she is afraid that the school has given up on Paul. Her greatest fear is that he will be sent to a residential facility where he will be physically restrained and mistreated.

Background Information:

From the first year of his life, it was clear to Paul's parents that he was different from other children. He cried about 6 hours a day, sometimes more, from 2 months of age to almost 2 years of age. His cries were such that his parents felt he was in terrible pain. They took him from doctor to doctor trying to uncover the source of his discomfort. When Paul was 20 months old, one of these doctors told the parents that they would just have to learn to live with the crying because there was no physical cause that could be treated. The next day, Mr. Wender left. He filed for a divorce shortly thereafter. He has had no contact with his son since that time. Mrs. Wender continued to seek help from the medical community. Around the age of 2 years, Paul's crying diminished somewhat. This brought his mother some relief, but then she began to be distressed by other behaviors he started demonstrating. For example, he stopped making eye contact with anyone, including her. It was as if Paul looked through people as opposed to looking at them. He began insisting that everything in his room and most of the house be situated in the same way he left it. If he lined up two dozen dominoes on the living room floor, he wanted them left in that position. Mrs. Wender soon found that it was easier to leave things the way Paul wanted them rather than face the extreme behavioral outbursts that resulted from moving his things. By the time Paul was 2 years old, he had been diagnosed with severe autism.

Mrs. Wender's life has revolved around her son and his needs. Her friends have accused her of being a martyr for Paul. They believe he should have been institutionalized many years ago, so she could have some life of her own. Mrs. Wender has been involved in parent support groups for families who have children with autism for many years. She has heard nightmarish stories of children who were institutionalized and ended up either in a drugged stupor or in physical restraints in facilities that were understaffed and unable to meet the needs of any child, let alone one with needs like Paul's. She knows that Paul's behavior and his size make him a candidate for such

© 2005 by PRO-ED, Inc. All rights reserved. Duplicating this page is strictly prohibited.

a placement. She is also uncertain about how much longer she can control his behavior in her own home. Mrs. Wender lives in fear that one of his outbursts will result in him throwing a chair through the living room window or something worse. She knows Paul will never be able to live in a group home situation, not unless his behavior changes drastically. Her only hope is that Middleton High School will continue to keep him and provide him with the full-time aide that allows him some degree of inclusion.

Case Study Activity

Individual or Group Case Analysis

Answer the following questions and be prepared to discuss them in class.

1. Do you consider Paul's current educational placement and circumstances to be inclusive? In your opinion, is the use of a full-time paraprofessional justified for this one student?

_____

_____

_____

_____

_____

_____

_____

2. Do you think Paul should be excluded from physical education? Should Paul have his lunch in the special education classroom instead of the school lunchroom? Should he be moved to a special school or institution at this point?

_____

_____

_____

_____

_____

_____

_____

© 2005 by PRO-ED, Inc. All rights reserved. Duplicating this page is strictly prohibited.

3. If you were Mrs. Yates, how would you handle parent complaints regarding the two recent incidents of Paul's aggressive behavior?

_____

_____

_____

_____

_____

_____

_____

4. What strategies might be implemented to diminish Paul's aggressive behavior?

_____

_____

_____

_____

_____

_____

_____

5. What is the prognosis for Paul? Is there anything the school can do to support Mrs. Wender in her efforts to keep her son in her home and community?

_____

_____

_____

_____

_____

_____

_____

© 2005 by PRO-ED, Inc. All rights reserved. Duplicating this page is strictly prohibited.

6. Create A Question (optional)

_____

_____

_____

_____

_____

_____

Veru

Veru is a 10-year-old child at Waltonville Elementary School. He was diagnosed with autism at the age of 3. Veru has been in a full-time special education class since he started school. This year, he is to be included in a general education fifth-grade classroom for half of the instructional day. He will have a paraprofessional with him for most of this time, except for 1 hour of math. The principal has reassigned Veru's paraprofessional during this time period because he needs her to assist with a difficult tube feeding for another child with very severe disabilities. Thus, Mr. Wang, his fifth-grade teacher, will not have any assistance during his math class. Mr. Wang is reluctant to have Veru in the classroom because of the distracting behaviors he displays. One of the most disturbing behaviors is that of head banging. Veru has built up a huge mass of scar tissue on his forehead from banging his head against all sorts of surfaces. Veru's parents, Mr. and Mrs. Kishore, have made it clear that they consider it the teacher's responsibility to keep Veru from engaging in this self-injurious behavior. Other behaviors that Veru demonstrates are head and face slapping, biting, and hand flapping. He also makes loud groaning noises that are very upsetting to Mr. Wang.

Mr. and Mrs. Kishore believe it is in Veru's best interests to be included in general education as much as possible. It is their opinion that Veru has much

more potential than he has been credited as having. They are especially interested in having the school personnel use facilitated communication to encourage his language development. Veru's paraprofessional has been trained in the use of facilitated communication. She has been working closely with him for several months now, but she has not had much success with this method of communication. Regardless of the limited progress, Mr. and Mrs. Kishore have requested that the keyboard be used throughout the day. Their expectation is that Mr. Wang will also use it during math class when Veru's paraprofessional is not available. They have suggested to him that he could benefit from the facilitated communication training class that is sponsored by a local university. They have also suggested that Mr. Wang take a sign language class, as Veru uses about 20 basic signs, and they are hoping to see more growth in that area of communication. Mr. Wang cannot imagine undertaking a special course of training on his own time to benefit only one student in his class. As politely as possible, he has declined.

Mr. Wang has told the principal, Mr. Bridges, that he would prefer that Veru be placed in one of the other fifth-grade classes with a teacher who perhaps has more experience and patience dealing with children like Veru. Mr. Bridges replied that because Mr.

© 2005 by PRO-ED, Inc. All rights reserved. Duplicating this page is strictly prohibited.

CASE STUDIES

Wang is the only male teacher in the fifth grade and has the most disciplined classroom in the building, he is the obvious choice to deal with children with behavioral problems. The principal also reminded Mr. Wang that the Kishores are close friends of the superintendent. He has suggested that a conference be held with the Kishores to talk about their expectations for this school year.

Background Information:

Mr. and Mrs. Kishore are both highly educated professionals. Mr. Kishore has a PhD in physics and works with NASA, while Mrs. Kishore is a medical doctor and a research oncologist. Both parents were in their mid-forties when Veru was born. Although Veru displayed very slow development and atypical social behaviors from the first year of life, the Kishores were reluctant to accept the notion that something could be wrong. One of his preschool teachers referred him to Child Find because the parents did not agree with the teacher's recommendation that they seek a developmental evaluation for Veru. The Kishores finally did agree to the evaluation. How-ever, they did not agree with the findings, which suggested that Veru's IQ fell into the moderate to severe range of mental retardation. They believe that Veru's severe language disorder has prevented him from demonstrating his full potential. They are very excited about the possibility that facilitated communication may provide their son with the means of communication that has eluded him thus far.

The Kishores always felt it was a mistake to place Veru with other children who had autism and mental retardation. They do not understand how he could possibly be challenged in that kind of an environment. Although they have tremendous respect for Mrs. Delgado, Veru's special education teacher, they really feel that Veru belongs in the mainstream with other children. Mrs. Delgado serves as the secretary for the local chapter of the National Autism Society, so she and the Kishores often find themselves working together for this organization. Mrs. Delgado is not sure that she agrees with the idea of including this student in the mainstream for half of the instructional day, but she is willing to provide as much support as she can to Veru and his family.

 Case Study Activity

Individual or Group Case Analysis

Answer the following questions and be prepared to discuss them in class.

1. What are the benefits of placing Veru in a general education class? What are some of the curriculum barriers Veru will experience in this environment? How could assistive technology support this student's learning?

_____

_____

_____

_____

_____

_____

_____

© 2005 by PRO-ED, Inc. All rights reserved. Duplicating this page is strictly prohibited.

2. What should Mr. Wang do to decrease Veru's head banging? How can he manage this behavior while he is teaching math class?

_____

_____

_____

_____

_____

_____

_____

3. Should Mr. Wang be responsible for using facilitated communication during math class? If you were Mr. Wang, would you try to learn sign language and facilitated communication in the training courses suggested by the parents? Do you think this family expects too much from the classroom teacher?

_____

_____

_____

_____

_____

_____

_____

_____

4. Do you agree with Mr. Bridges's idea that Mr. Wang should have Veru in his classroom because he is the only male teacher at Waltonville and a strong disciplinarian? How should these placement decisions be made by the school administration?

_____

_____

_____

_____

_____

_____

_____

© 2005 by PRO-ED, Inc. All rights reserved. Duplicating this page is strictly prohibited.

CASE STUDIES

5. How can the teachers work with this family to maximize Veru's success in school? Give four strategies.

_____

_____

_____

_____

_____

_____

_____

_____

6. Create A Question (optional)

_____

_____

_____

_____

_____

_____

_____

© 2005 by PRO-ED, Inc. All rights reserved. Duplicating this page is strictly prohibited.

CHAPTER 8

Sensory Impairments

Emilio

Emilio is a 9-year-old third grader at Mountain View Elementary. He has a bilateral mixed hearing loss that falls into the moderate to severe range. Emilio's hearing loss is thought to be related to a bout of meningitis, which occurred at the age of 13 months, and to frequent episodes of otitis media during the preschool years. His parents, Mr. and Mrs. Salinas, are not deaf. Emilio has four school-age siblings, all of whom are hearing. This will be Emilio's first year at Mountain View. His family has moved from a large city to this rural setting in the mountains. When Emilio lived in the city, he attended a center school for children with hearing impairments. The approach used by this school was total communication, which meant that Emilio was taught American Sign Language (ASL) in addition to his speech and language therapy. Mr. and Mrs. Salinas were dissatisfied with Emilio's previous school program. They have decided that they do not want their son to continue to learn ASL. They feel that it isolates Emilio from their family. At one time, the family made an effort to learn ASL, but after a brief period, they discovered how difficult it was and gave up.

Mr. Issacs, the principal of Mountain View Elementary, has been very welcoming to Emilio and his family. He explained to the family that his school did not have a hearing impairment program, but he felt that they could meet Emilio's educational needs. There is such a program at the neighboring school, which is 30 miles down the road. Mr. and Mrs. Salinas were told that if they chose that school, bus service would be provided to Emilio. The family declined, saying that they wanted Emilio to be in his neighborhood school with his siblings. Although Mr. Issacs does not have much experience with serving the needs of children with hearing impairments, he is eager to work with this child and his family. Mountain View has a special education resource teacher, Mrs. Cartwright, who works with the other teachers to provide modifications for students with disabilities. Mr. Issacs feels confident that Mrs. Cartwright will be able to provide Emilio with the educational adaptations he needs to experience success.

Mr. and Mrs. Salinas met with Mr. Issacs and Mrs. Cartwright to discuss some of their concerns be-fore the scheduled IEP meeting. Emilio's achievement test scores reveal that his reading and written expression are on a mid–first-grade level, whereas his math is at approximately the late–second-grade level. Computations have been identified as a strength, and problem solving has been identified as a weakness. Mr. and Mrs. Salinas are also concerned with Emilio's socialization. Although he had several good friends in the hearing impaired program at his previous school, he has never had a hearing friend. This is very upsetting to the family. Additionally, the parents referred to the problem of Emilio turning off his hearing aid. He has complained to his family that the hearing aid is uncomfortable and makes a disturbing sound, but his family has had it checked and rechecked. Emilio's doctors and his audiologist have strongly suggested that Emilio keep this aid on, because it is their feeling that it will maximize his residual hearing and help him in the classroom. As Emilio's speech is difficult to comprehend, speech therapy is a service that the family wants to continue along with speech reading. Neither of the parents wants Emilio to continue learning sign language. They want to shift from a total communication approach to an oralist approach.

Background Information:

Emilio's parents and grandparents were born in Mexico. Emilio's maternal grandparents live with the Salinases, so Spanish is frequently spoken in the home environment. Mr. and Mrs. Salinas want their children to be fluent in the language of their native country, but they also believe that their children must have good English language skills because they see this as a prerequisite to success in the United States. They are worried that Emilio will not be skilled in either language.

When Emilio's hearing impairment was identified at the age of 3, his parents had no understanding of the different types of problems he might encounter. They enrolled him in a preschool classroom that was part of a special education school for children with disabilities. Mr. and Mrs. Salinas did not like this school experience. Many of the children who attended this school had severe disabilities and were limited in their physical mobility and communica-

© 2005 by PRO-ED, Inc. All rights reserved. Duplicating this page is strictly prohibited.

CASE STUDIES

tion. However, they did not realize that they might have another choice for their son. After 2 years in this special preschool, Emilio was moved to a school that was closer to his neighborhood. This school was considered to be the center school for children with significant hearing impairments. The principal and the teacher both described Emilio's new program as being inclusive, providing him with many opportunities to socialize with the other children in the school. But as far as Mr. and Mrs. Salinas could see, this socialization never happened for Emilio or any of the other children with hearing impairments. The program used a total communication approach to deaf education. The elementary school also had a sign language program that taught ASL to the children without disabil-

ities. But something seemed to be missing. Whenever Mrs. Salinas visited the school to have lunch with Emilio or to assist with playground duty, she always observed the same thing: The children who were deaf would play together on the playground and sit together in the lunchroom. She never saw Emilio or any of the other students who were deaf interact with the hearing students. When she discussed these concerns with the teacher of the program, she was told that Emilio did socialize with the hearing students and that integration was not a problem in that school. In the 2 years that Emilio was there, he was never invited to a hearing child's home, and Mrs. Salinas never heard him refer to any friends other than those in the special education program.

Case Study Activity

Individual or Group Case Analysis

Answer the following questions and be prepared to discuss them in class.

1. Do you think Emilio should discontinue ASL instruction? Why or why not? Why do you think Emilio's family is so opposed to this instruction?

_____

_____

_____

_____

_____

_____

_____

_____

_____

© 2005 by PRO-ED, Inc. All rights reserved. Duplicating this page is strictly prohibited.

2. If you were Emilio's third-grade teacher at Mountain View, what general strategies would you implement to assist him in accessing the curriculum?

_____

_____

_____

_____

_____

_____

_____

3. Why do you think Emilio did not experience much socialization with students without disabilities at his previous school? How can his new school help him to achieve more success in this area? Give four specific strategies for increasing socialization.

_____

_____

_____

_____

_____

_____

_____

4. Why do you think Emilio is reading below grade level? Describe how you would approach reading instruction with this student. What types of assistive technology might be beneficial for improving his skills in this area?

_____

_____

_____

_____

_____

_____

_____

© 2005 by PRO-ED, Inc. All rights reserved. Duplicating this page is strictly prohibited.

5. Do you think the language background of Emilio's family will influence his acquisition of the English language? Explain your response.

_____

_____

_____

_____

_____

_____

6. Create A Question (optional)

_____

_____

_____

_____

_____

Jake

Jake is a 14-year-old freshman at Walker High School. He has been profoundly deaf since shortly after birth as a result of cytomegalovirus. Jake is able to use his voice for communication only on a limited basis, because it is difficult for others to understand him. He has the benefit of an interpreter for algebra, English, and biology classes. Jake is an excellent speech reader who has been doing fairly well since he started at Walker High this fall. His first report card indicated that he was progressing in a satisfactory manner. He received mostly Cs with a B+ in biology. His parents, Mr. and Mrs. Penrod, are pleased with the way things are going.

Although Jake's teachers are not concerned about his academic progress, they are somewhat concerned about his emotional state. He always seems withdrawn, and he does not appear to have any friends. Mr. Keefe, who does quite a bit of cooperative learning in his social studies class, has noticed that Jake rarely participates in these group activities. Mrs. Kuhn, Jake's biology teacher, has observed that Jake does not seem interested in working with his lab partner. In fact, Jake's lab partner has complained to Mrs. Kuhn and has asked to be assigned to another partner. Apparently, Jake does all of the work and then expects his partner to copy the answers from him. He does not show any interest in cooperative problem solving.

© 2005 by PRO-ED, Inc. All rights reserved. Duplicating this page is strictly prohibited.

Background Information:

Jake started preschool at the age of 3 in a special education program for children with hearing impairments. Following this preschool experience, he attended a self-contained special education program in an elementary school that had a center for students with hearing impairments. He stayed in this program for 6 years. When he was ready to go on to middle school, his parents asked that he be mainstreamed. The school district supported this placement because they were in the process of moving toward inclusion for all special education students. They also agreed to hire a half-time interpreter for Jake to assist in this transition.

During the 3 years that Jake spent in middle school, he began to demonstrate behavioral problems. He started skipping school and was apprehended for shoplifting. He also started showing signs of withdrawal and depression. The students who had been his peers during the elementary school years had either been transferred to other neighborhood middle schools or to the state school for students with visual and hearing impairments, which is 100 miles away. Jake's parents took him to see a psychologist, who diagnosed him as having an adjustment reaction. He recommended therapy, but Jake refused to go. It was at this time that Jake first brought up the idea of transferring to the state residential school. Mr. and Mrs. Penrod were surprised and dismayed at this idea. They are against the notion that deaf students can be better educated in a segregated setting. They are firmly committed to the idea that all people need to learn to live together in an integrated community. They are not interested in having their son spend more time communicating with sign language. They know that the state school uses the American Sign Language (ASL) approach to education, and they believe that Jake should spend more time attempting to use his speech for communication purposes. Jake's parents worry that he would be tempted to give up on using speech altogether if he were given that option.

Jake's interpreter, Mrs. Lucero, supports the idea of the transfer to the state school. She has commented several times that Jake appears to be lonely at Walker High School. She feels that he has decided he just does not fit in with the other adolescents in the mainstream. Mrs. Lucero's parents and two siblings are deaf, so she has a different perspective on Jake's situation. On one occasion she mentioned that Jake was missing out on the "experience of the Deaf culture," which could help him have more insight regarding the choices available to him.

Case Study Activity

Individual or Group Case Analysis

Answer the following questions and be prepared to discuss them in class.

1. If you were Jake's social studies teacher, how would you encourage his participation in cooperative learning activities for that class?

_____

_____

_____

_____

_____

_____

© 2005 by PRO-ED, Inc. All rights reserved. Duplicating this page is strictly prohibited.

2. What would you do about Jake's lab partner if you were the biology teacher?

_____

_____

_____

_____

_____

_____

_____

_____

3. What is Mrs. Lucero referring to when she says that Jake is missing out on the "Deaf culture"? Why might she think that segregated education is preferable to his current integrated education?

_____

_____

_____

_____

_____

_____

_____

_____

_____

4. Why does Jake want to go to the school for students with hearing impairments? Could this be described as an expression of adolescent independence?

_____

_____

_____

_____

_____

_____

_____

_____

© 2005 by PRO-ED, Inc. All rights reserved. Duplicating this page is strictly prohibited.

5. Why does it seem so important for the Penrods to keep Jake at Walker High School? Give four possible reasons. Where do you think Jake should go to school? Why?

_____

_____

_____

_____

_____

_____

_____

6. Create A Question (optional)

_____

_____

_____

_____

_____

_____

_____

Karen

Karen is a 17-year-old senior at Cannonville High School. She has retinitis pigmentosa, a genetic eye disease that progressively leads to blindness. Karen had been using large print books for the past 3 years, but her visual impairment has recently worsened to the extent that she is no longer able to read print of any size. Ms. Ziebert, the special education resource teacher at Cannonville High, has been providing Karen with adapted materials since Karen started school there. Ms. Ziebert has also been in charge of collaborating with Karen's other teachers to ensure her success. However, there has actually been very little collaboration because Karen has been able to do everything that her peers have done with few exceptions. This year will be different. Karen's parents, Mr. and Mrs. James, have informed Ms. Ziebert that a recent eye exam determined that Karen's vision had degenerated to 20/400 in her right eye and 20/450 in her left eye. The ophthalmologist has predicted that Karen's residual vision will be minimal by the end of this year. He has recommended that Karen learn Braille.

Karen flatly refuses to have anything to do with Braille. She wants to continue to go to her classes and

© 2005 by PRO-ED, Inc. All rights reserved. Duplicating this page is strictly prohibited.

CASE STUDIES

learn as well as she can without any intervention. She feels that she can keep up with her studies by concentrating harder on the auditory aspects of instruction. Karen is struggling to keep her life as normal as possible. She wants to continue to be a member of the cheerleading squad, even though her parents want her to quit. It is very important for her to keep up with her friends. She and her boyfriend recently broke up—it was the boyfriend who initiated the split, and Karen suspects it had something to do with her failing eyesight. Karen has told both her parents and Ms. Ziebert that she will not participate in mobility training. She indicated that she would rather spend the time studying for her driver's license exam.

Background Information:

Mr. and Mrs. James have known since Karen's birth that she had retinitis pigmentosa. Karen's maternal grandmother also had this progressive disease, as did her great-grandmother. Karen always said that she was not troubled by the disease because she felt her prognosis was very positive. Both her grand-

mother and great-grandmother did not become blind until they reached their 90s. Karen frequently commented that by the time she became blind she would not care because she would be too old to do anything anyway. Every year when Karen would have her annual or semiannual eye exam, the ophthalmologist would caution Karen that her sight was worsening, but Karen did not seem to believe him. Mr. and Mrs. James tried to help Karen come to terms with what was happening; however, they could not make any inroads. They even took her to a psychologist, hoping that this would help her prepare for whatever lay ahead. Karen stood firm in her refusal to believe that the prognosis for her eye disease would be different from that of her grandmother and great-grandmother. The psychologist told Mr. and Mrs. James that she felt Karen was depressed. Karen denied this. She claims to be a "happy, carefree teen," but her parents think otherwise. Karen also denies losing weight, even though her mother knows that she has lost at least 5 pounds in the past 6 months.

Case Study Activity

Individual or Group Case Analysis

Answer the following questions and be prepared to discuss them in class.

1. Is it reasonable to expect Karen to learn Braille at this point in her schooling? What types of assistive technology could provide assistance to Karen?

_____

_____

_____

_____

_____

_____

© 2005 by PRO-ED, Inc. All rights reserved. Duplicating this page is strictly prohibited.

2. Is it possible that Karen could succeed in her classes without any intervention? If you were one of Karen's teachers in the general education curriculum, how would you help Karen adjust to her new situation?

_____

_____

_____

_____

_____

_____

_____

3. Should Karen follow her parents' advice and give up the cheerleading squad? Why do her parents think this is a good idea? What is Karen's perspective?

_____

_____

_____

_____

_____

_____

_____

_____

4. If you were Ms. Ziebert, what would your priorities be in terms of working with Karen? How would you accomplish these objectives?

_____

_____

_____

_____

_____

_____

_____

© 2005 by PRO-ED, Inc. All rights reserved. Duplicating this page is strictly prohibited.

CASE STUDIES

5. Does Karen need mobility training? Does the fact that she has been attending this school for the past 3 years, when she had her sight, have anything to do with the amount or type of training she will need?

_____

_____

_____

_____

_____

_____

_____

_____

6. Create A Question (optional)

_____

_____

_____

_____

_____

_____

_____

_____

_____

Lauren

Lauren is a 13-year-old seventh grader at Woodlawn Middle School who has recently transferred from another state. Although Lauren has an inherited bilateral sensorineural hearing loss in the severe to profound range, she is able to use her voice for communication purposes. Most of her speech is intelligible, and she is also an excellent speech reader. At her previous school, Lauren had a full-time sign language interpreter whom she shared with another adolescent who was deaf. The situation worked out well because the school system placed both of the girls in the same classes with the interpreter. Lauren's other school was

© 2005 by PRO-ED, Inc. All rights reserved. Duplicating this page is strictly prohibited.

located in a large metropolitan area, whereas Woodlawn Middle School was in a rural area.

Lauren is an attractive adolescent who is also a very bright and caring individual. She was well thought of at her other school, and although she has been at Woodlawn for only a few weeks, it appears that she has made a good adjustment. She is also doing well academically. Her English teacher was so impressed by her first paper that she encouraged her to join the staff of the school newspaper as a reporter. Lauren has received Bs on all of her geometry quizzes and a B+ on her first civics test. She works with the speech therapist for 30 minutes twice a week and has access to the learning lab when she needs help with her assignments.

When Lauren's parents, Mr. and Mrs. Baylor, who are both deaf, came to school for the IEP meeting, they were provided an interpreter because neither of them speak. During that conference, school personnel reviewed the previous goals and discussed Lauren's educational goals. The parents asked why Lauren's sign language interpreter was not present at the IEP meeting. It was at this point that the pupil assessment team informed the parents that Lauren would not have an interpreter at Woodlawn Middle School. When the team evaluated Lauren, they concluded that she had the capability to achieve without an interpreter because of her strong speech reading and oral language ability. Mr. and Mrs. Baylor were very distraught. They insisted that in order for Lauren to be able to achieve according to her full potential, she would require the services of an interpreter. Lauren interjected at this point, saying that she was doing fine and things were different here because she was the only deaf student in the school and it would not make any sense for her to have an interpreter all to herself. Mr. Baylor quickly signed a message to Lauren that surprised her, as well as the interpreter. It was obvious that Lauren was going to be in big trouble when she got home. Lauren did not say anything more for the rest of the meeting. The Baylors refused to sign the IEP. It is their position that Lauren would be a straight-A student with the help of an interpreter. They will not consider her educational program to be appropriate if she makes only Bs and Cs, which they are certain will happen if she does not get the help she needs.

Background Information:

Mr. and Mrs. Baylor are both congenitally deaf. Neither of them had a pleasant school experience. Mrs. Baylor's school experience was dismal until she convinced her parents that she should go to the state residential school for children with hearing impairments. Mr. Baylor struggled through the public school system until he was 15 years old and then dropped out. He was the object of considerable ridicule by many of his hearing classmates. Because he was never able to use his voice for communication purposes, he was socially isolated from his peers. He also felt that his teachers always considered him to be less intellectually able because he was deaf. It was Mr. Baylor's dream to become a lawyer, but he soon realized that he would never have the educational opportunities to fulfill that dream. Mr. Baylor became very successful as a businessman later in life, but he has never forgotten his painful school experiences. He is determined that his daughter will be given the educational opportunities that he missed.

© 2005 by PRO-ED, Inc. All rights reserved. Duplicating this page is strictly prohibited.

CASE STUDIES

Case Study Activity

Individual or Group Activity

Answer the following questions and be prepared to discuss them in class.

1. Does Lauren have a legal right to a full-time interpreter? Because her previous school district provided her with this service, does this mean that Woodlawn must do the same? What laws might influence this case?

_____

_____

_____

_____

_____

_____

2. Do you think Lauren should be given a full-time interpreter? Are there other interventions, such as assistive devices, that could assist Lauren in accessing the general education curriculum?

_____

_____

_____

_____

_____

_____

3. How could the school work with Mr. and Mrs. Baylor to resolve this difference of opinion regarding Lauren's needs? What will happen if the Baylors refuse to sign the IEP?

_____

_____

_____

_____

_____

_____

© 2005 by PRO-ED, Inc. All rights reserved. Duplicating this page is strictly prohibited.

4. Will Lauren's needs change as she moves to high school? What kinds of supports would she need to ensure her success when she makes the transition from middle school to high school?

_____

_____

_____

_____

_____

_____

_____

5. Do you think there are significant differences in the quality and type of special education services that are provided in different school districts? What variables might influence these services?

_____

_____

_____

_____

_____

_____

_____

6. Create A Question (optional)

_____

_____

_____

_____

_____

_____

_____

© 2005 by PRO-ED, Inc. All rights reserved. Duplicating this page is strictly prohibited.

Ted

Ted is a 6-year-old kindergarten student in Mrs. Montoya's classroom. Ted has been blind since shortly after his birth due to retinopathy of prematurity. He did not attend preschool, so he does not have any structured school experience. Mrs. Montoya has never had a student with a visual impairment in her class. She really wants Ted to have a successful year, and she believes that it will be good for her other kindergarten students to have Ted as their peer. Ted is scheduled to spend the entire day in the classroom. For 30 minutes per day, he will have the services of a special education teacher, Mr. MacManus, who will be teaching Braille and mobility to Ted. For the rest of the day, Mrs. Montoya has been told that Ted will be learning the same curriculum as the other kindergartners. Mrs. Montoya has also been informed that increasing Ted's socialization with his peers has been specified as an important IEP goal for this beginning school year. Development of different types of listening skills—such as attentive, analytical, appreciative, and selective listening—has also been identified as an important preacademic goal.

Ted is a shy child with a charming personality. He is healthy, but he gives the appearance of being fragile because he is small for his age and pale compared to the other children. Mrs. Montoya was immediately won over by his sweet disposition and sense of humor. She carefully positioned his desk in the middle of the classroom surrounded by students whom she knew would provide assistance until Ted could navigate the classroom independently. During the first week, she developed a plan whereby Ted would have a friend assigned to him every day for recess and lunch. This friend would help Ted get used to the playground, cafeteria, and restroom. Since all the kindergartners are assigned a classroom chore, she assigned Ted the chore of picking up books in the reading corner and reshelving them.

When Ted's mother, Mrs. Shields, heard about Mrs. Montoya's plans for increasing socialization, she was less than enthusiastic. She told Mrs. Montoya that she did not want Ted to be on the playground without the direct supervision of an adult. Mrs. Shields fur-ther told her that without that type of supervision, she was afraid that Ted would be hit by a swing or a baseball or would be involved in some other playground accident. She was upset when she discovered that her son's desk was in the middle of the room instead of being next to the teacher's. And she also did not like the idea of assigning Ted a classroom chore, saying, "It should be obvious that my son can't do all of the things the other students are expected to do—he should be getting more help for his school work instead of cleaning up the room." Mrs. Shields told Mrs. Montoya that if she did not feel that she had the time to provide Ted with more help and supervision, she would request another kindergarten classroom where the teacher could.

Background Information:

Mr. and Mrs. Shields are both professionals, and Ted is their only child. When he was born 10 weeks premature, they were in a state of shock. They felt ill-prepared to deal with the numerous medical problems confronting their son. Mrs. Shields quit her job and began devoting herself full time to her son's recovery. When they were told that Ted would be blind, Mrs. Shields had to be medicated for an anxiety disorder. With time, the Shields were able to accept Ted's disability and became dedicated to fulfilling his needs. Mrs. Shields did not send him to preschool because she was afraid he would be hurt on the playground or the teacher would have no idea how to work with him. Instead, Mrs. Shields began researching visual impairments and provided Ted with a preschool curriculum in the home environment. She considered home schooling Ted instead of sending him to public kindergarten, but Mr. Shields was against it. He feels that Ted is lonely and needs peer interaction. Mrs. Shields would prefer that this socialization take place later, when Ted is physically larger and less fragile. Ted's father argues that he is a normal child who only looks fragile because he spends all of his time indoors and does not get the exercise he needs. Ted's pediatrician agrees.

© 2005 by PRO-ED, Inc. All rights reserved. Duplicating this page is strictly prohibited.

Case Study Activity

Individual or Group Case Analysis

Answer the following questions and be prepared to discuss them in class.

1. What do you think about Mrs. Montoya's beginning plans for Ted's socialization? Will these place Ted in dangerous situations? If you were Ted's teacher, how would you facilitate socialization?

_____

_____

_____

_____

_____

_____

2. Is Ted ready for the transition from home to kindergarten? Should a child like Ted be home schooled until he is more physically fit and less likely to be injured at school?

_____

_____

_____

_____

_____

_____

3. Will Mrs. Montoya be expected to learn Braille? What types of assistive technology might enhance Ted's learning in the general education classroom?

_____

_____

_____

_____

_____

_____

© 2005 by PRO-ED, Inc. All rights reserved. Duplicating this page is strictly prohibited.

4. What will Mr. MacManus be teaching Ted with regard to mobility? What strategies might he use?

_____

_____

_____

_____

_____

_____

_____

_____

5. How can Mrs. Montoya and Mrs. Shields reach a compromise that will benefit Ted? Could better transition planning have made Ted's first experience less stressful for this family? How could this have been accomplished?

_____

_____

_____

_____

_____

_____

_____

_____

6. Create A Question (optional)

_____

_____

_____

_____

_____

_____

_____

_____

© 2005 by PRO-ED, Inc. All rights reserved. Duplicating this page is strictly prohibited.

Valerie

Valerie is a 10-year-old fourth grader at Desert Elementary School. Valerie's family has recently moved to the area from a large city in a neighboring state. At her previous school, Valerie spent most of the instructional day in a resource room where she was provided assistance from a vision specialist. Valerie has been identified as a student with low vision; her right eye is her best eye at 20/180, whereas her left eye is at 20/200. At Desert Elementary, there are no other students with visual impairments. This school is designated as a full-inclusion school, meaning that there are no special education resource or self-contained programs. The principal, Ms. Vanatta, has assured Valerie's mother, Mrs. Kemp, that Valerie will have the services of an itinerant vision specialist who will be collaborating with her classroom teacher to ensure that appropriate modifications are made for her.

It has been 2 months since Valerie started at Desert Elementary, and she has yet to see her vision teacher. Ms. Vanatta called Mrs. Kemp and told her that there would be a delay in getting services for Valerie because the vision specialist is out on maternity leave, but she would be returning shortly. When Mrs. Kemp objected, she was told that there was only one vision specialist for the county, so nothing could be done until she came back to work. When Mrs. Kemp asked if Valerie could get help from an occupational therapist, as she did in her previous school, Ms. Vanatta told her that would not be possible until they held Valerie's IEP meeting which, of course, could not occur until the vision teacher was back at school. Mrs. Kemp did not want to cause trouble in Valerie's new school, so she decided not to say anything more.

Meanwhile, it seemed that Valerie was becoming very unhappy. She was complaining of terrible headaches when she came home from school each day. She told her mother that she hated her new school and that she did not have any friends. Valerie also told Mrs. Kemp that she did not want to go to physical education class ever again because the teacher was so mean to her. Mrs. Kemp decided that she had better go to the school and find out what was going on.

She made an appointment to meet with Mrs. Ames, Valerie's fourth-grade teacher. When she arrived for the conference, she could not help noticing that Valerie's desk was at the back of the classroom. She told Mrs. Ames that Valerie had to have her desk in the front row. Mrs. Ames replied that she used a rotation system for moving the desks around in the classroom so that every student would have the opportunity to sit in the front row. She further told Mrs. Kemp that she did not need to worry about Valerie, because she was one of the brightest students in the class and it did not seem to matter where she sat, most of her work was excellent. There were a few areas of concern that Mrs. Ames did address. Although Valerie was considered to be a straight-A student in most subject areas, Mrs. Ames stated that she would most likely be getting a D in penmanship because of illegible handwriting. Mrs. Ames expressed concern that Valerie was not socializing well with her peers. She also mentioned that Valerie had difficulty staying in her seat; she was frequently away from her desk, moving around the room when she was supposed to be working. When Mrs. Kemp asked Mrs. Ames if she was aware that Valerie had a significant vision problem, Mrs. Ames said that she did notice that Valerie was "cross-eyed" and she had a habit of "flicking" her eyes that was distracting. By this point, Mrs. Kemp was starting to get angry. She tried to explain that Valerie was almost legally blind and that the distracting eye flicking that Mrs. Ames described was an involuntary eye movement referred to as nystagmus. Mrs. Ames replied that she had a hard time believing that Valerie had a vision problem when she did not even wear glasses. Mrs. Kemp continued to discuss Valerie's vision needs, but she had the distinct impression that Mrs. Ames was not really listening. Mrs. Ames told her that she had to end the conference because she had a doctor's appointment for which she could not be late. In parting, she told Mrs. Kemp that she should not worry about Valerie's academics; instead, she should spend her efforts helping her daughter make new friends. Mrs. Ames suggested that a soccer team might be just the thing for Valerie.

Mrs. Kemp had intended to visit the physical education teacher, but Mrs. Ames advised against it. She said, "Let me give you some advice. Mr. Ledbetter runs a pretty tight ship, and he doesn't take kindly to parents telling him how to teach his classes. If you want your daughter to have a chance in his class, you had better let the two of them work

© 2005 by PRO-ED, Inc. All rights reserved. Duplicating this page is strictly prohibited.

CASE STUDIES

out their own problems." Mrs. Kemp is now extremely angry and upset, but she is not sure what to do. She is wondering what her next step should be. She is starting to think she should call her brother, who is an attorney.

Background Information:

Valerie was involved in a car accident when she was 3 weeks old. Her mother had taken her out of the car seat to feed her just before the accident occurred. Valerie sustained a head injury, but the doctors were unsure about the effects. To this day, the doctors do not know whether Valerie's vision problems occurred as a result of the accident or whether she was born with an eye defect. She has had numerous operations for the strabismus, but Valerie's eyes are still not aligned. The nystagmus developed shortly after 6 months of age. From Valerie's preschool years, many different types of lenses have been prescribed for her, but they have all caused her to have severe headaches and have not helped with her vision. She needs enlarged print, which she then reads from a near point distance of approximately 4 inches.

Valerie had visual–motor difficulties from the beginning. When Valerie was an infant, she could not perform such activities as transferring a rattle from her left hand to her right hand. Her occupational therapist referred to Valerie's problems in this area as being the result of a major "sensory integration deficit." She could not throw a ball until the second grade. Valerie still cannot hop on one foot or skip, nor has she ever learned to ride a bike or roller-skate. At her previous school, Valerie had occupational therapy on a daily basis and adaptive physical education. Her IEP goals for these areas were extensive.

Valerie has always had a difficult time with socialization. Because of her vision problems, she cannot recognize faces until the individual is standing within a foot of her. But through the years, Valerie did make some good friends, many of whom were her classmates in the gifted program at her previous school. It took a long time to establish these friendships, but they were lasting relationships. Several of her old friends still call and write to Valerie. It saddens Mrs. Kemp to see Valerie struggle to make new friends at Desert Elementary.

Case Study Activities

Part I:
Role Playing

Break into groups of five students and assume one of the following roles: Mrs. Kemp, Mr. Henslow (Mrs. Kemp's brother), Mrs. Ames, Ms. Vanatta, and Mr. Ledbetter. Simulate a meeting in which the group attempts to resolve this problem. Following this activity, write a summary of the resolution.

Resolution

_____

_____

_____

_____

_____

© 2005 by PRO-ED, Inc. All rights reserved. Duplicating this page is strictly prohibited.

Part II:
Individual or Group Case Analysis

Answer the following questions and be prepared to discuss them in class.

1. Is it legal for the principal to say that Valerie will not have any services until her vision teacher comes back from maternity leave? What laws might influence this particular situation? What should have been done in this situation?

\
\
\
\
\
\
\

2. If Valerie had friends at her previous school, why is she having problems making friends at Desert Elementary? What strategies could Mrs. Ames use to facilitate her socialization at her new school?

\
\
\
\
\
\
\

3. Why do you think Valerie has such a difficult time with visual–motor activities? What kinds of adaptations should be made for Valerie in her physical education class?

\
\
\
\
\
\
\

© 2005 by PRO-ED, Inc. All rights reserved. Duplicating this page is strictly prohibited.

CASE STUDIES

4. Because Valerie is doing so well in school, is it possible that Mrs. Ames is right in believing that she does not require any modifications?

_____

_____

_____

_____

_____

_____

_____

5. If you were Mrs. Ames, what interventions would you implement in the fourth-grade classroom to assist this student in accessing the curriculum? How could assistive technology be used to support Valerie's learning?

_____

_____

_____

_____

_____

_____

_____

6. Create A Question (optional)

_____

_____

_____

_____

_____

_____

_____

_____

© 2005 by PRO-ED, Inc. All rights reserved. Duplicating this page is strictly prohibited.

CHAPTER 9

Gifted and Talented

Jeffrey

Jeffrey is an 8-year-old child in the fourth grade at Fosterville Elementary School. His mother, Ms. Cates, recognized him as functioning well above his pre-school peers, so she asked the school district to waive the requirement that states all children must be 5 years of age by September 15th in order to begin kindergarten. She wanted Jeffrey to start school even though he would not be 5 years old until October 10th. The school district refused to do this, so Jeffrey had to wait another year to start school. As soon as Jeffrey started kindergarten, his teacher recognized that his abilities were well above that of the other children. He was tested during his kindergarten year and determined to be a "highly gifted" child. Because Fosterville did not have a gifted program suitable for meeting Jeffrey's needs, the school decided to allow him to skip both first and second grades in an effort to provide him with a more intellectually stimulating environment. His teachers agreed that he probably should have skipped third grade also, but they felt that his social needs would go unmet if he progressed that rapidly through the school years.

Ms. Cates felt that Jeffrey went through third grade in a state of complete boredom. She thought that his enrichment program was also a waste of time. The teacher for this program would meet with the children once a week and assign them a project, supposedly based on their interests. She would then review their progress on this project during enrichment time for the next 3 weeks until the assignment was due. The enrichment teacher did not seem to have any interest in Jeffrey's projects, which usually dealt with mechanical engineering, nor did she seem to have any ability to guide him in his ideas. By the time Jeffrey had finished third grade, it appeared to Ms. Cates that he had lost a lot of his interest and enthusiasm for school and learning. His mother is determined that fourth grade will be more stimulating for her son.

When she spoke to Mrs. Lewis, the fourth-grade teacher, at the beginning of the school year, she carefully explained her concerns regarding her son's schooling and the expectations she had for this school year. She felt that Mrs. Lewis largely ignored her concerns and turned the discussion around to focus on Jeffrey's needs for socialization. Mrs. Lewis told her that the third-grade teacher described Jeffrey as a "social isolate" who really had no friends at school. She suggested that this should be an area of focus for Jeffrey's fourth-grade year. Ms. Cates is aware that Jeffrey does not have many friends at school, but Jeffrey explains this by saying he is just not interested in the same things that his peers find interesting.

Mrs. Lewis stated that Jeffrey's third-grade teacher told her that Jeffrey has a morbid interest in tragic events reported in the news. She advised Ms. Cates to keep him away from the television and newspaper when something tragic has transpired, as a means of dealing with that behavior. Ms. Cates was aghast at Mrs. Lewis' interpretation of this aspect of Jeffrey's behavior. Jeffrey appears to focus on tragic events because he is more sensitive to issues of ethics, morality, and evil than his peers, who do not fully understand many of these issues at this point in their development. Ms. Cates cannot believe that Mrs. Lewis could have such an interpretation of Jeffrey's sensitivity. She also cannot believe that the third-grade teacher said all these negative things about Jeffrey to Mrs. Lewis, and yet never mentioned anything to her. She found herself getting too emotional to continue the conference.

On the way home, in the car, Ms. Cates started crying and could not stop. She feels that Jeffrey does not have a chance to get an appropriate education for his needs in that school. She wishes she could send him to the Gates School for the Gifted, a private school with the best reputation in the city and a yearly tuition of $15,000. As a single mother, she is doing all she can to meet the family's basic needs. There is seldom any money left over for anything except an occasional movie or trip to the museum. Sometimes, she feels that Jeffrey's intellect is more of a burden than a gift. And today, she is feeling like a bad parent because she cannot get her son the help he needs from the school system.

Background Information:

Jeffrey's father and mother were never married. They had been engaged for a brief period of time, but the relationship soured when Jeffrey's mother became

© 2005 by PRO-ED, Inc. All rights reserved. Duplicating this page is strictly prohibited.

CASE STUDIES

pregnant. Even though Jeffrey's father lives in a neighboring town, he has never seen Jeffrey or taken any interest in establishing a relationship with him. Ms. Cates feels responsible for not providing her son with a father, even though she has tried everything she could to continue the relationship. Ms. Cates knows that Jeffrey comprehends and internalizes this rejection with an understanding well above his age. It makes her very sad that such a wonderful child is not appreciated and loved by both parents. She also feels that if Jeffrey had a "real father," there would be two people to provide for him, making it more plausible for Jeffrey to go to a private school and get the kind of education he needs.

Case Study Activity

Individual or Group Case Analysis

Answer the following questions and be prepared to discuss them in class.

1. Do you agree with the school district's policy of having a specific birth date requirement for entrance to kindergarten? Should the school district allow exceptions?

_____

_____

_____

_____

_____

_____

_____

2. Was it appropriate for Jeffrey's third-grade teacher to share her concerns about Jeffrey's social behavior with the fourth-grade teacher but not with his mother? Do you agree with Ms. Cates that Jeffrey's giftedness causes him to be more sensitive about ethics and morality? What does the literature on giftedness suggest about this topic?

_____

_____

_____

_____

_____

_____

© 2005 by PRO-ED, Inc. All rights reserved. Duplicating this page is strictly prohibited.

3. Do you think Jeffrey's enrichment program in the third grade was appropriate for his needs? In what ways could it have been modified to be more relevant for Jeffrey? Should Jeffrey have skipped third grade also? Why or why not?

_____

_____

_____

_____

_____

_____

_____

4. In your opinion, does Jeffrey have a socialization problem that should be addressed? Why or why not? Should socialization be the primary area of focus for Jeffrey in the fourth grade?

_____

_____

_____

_____

_____

_____

_____

5. If you were Jeffrey's teacher, how would you address his achievement needs? How could you use technology to support his learning? What other resources would you use?

_____

_____

_____

_____

_____

_____

_____

© 2005 by PRO-ED, Inc. All rights reserved. Duplicating this page is strictly prohibited.

CASE STUDIES

6. Create A Question (optional)

_____

_____

_____

_____

_____

_____

_____

Leo

Leo is a 15-year-old student at Carlton High School. He has been in the gifted program since he was in kindergarten, when his IQ was determined to be 165. He has completed all requirements for graduation and has taken his college boards—he scored in the 99th percentile on both the SAT and ACT. Leo desperately wants to go to college next year, but his parents, Mr. and Mrs. Demchak, have refused to agree to this plan. He has been accepted into the medical biomechanics program of a prestigious university located in New York. He has also been offered a full scholarship by this university. Mr. and Mrs. Demchak have stated that they think their son is too immature to go off to school by himself. They seem to understand that Leo is a highly creative individual, but they do not appear to trust him.

Leo's teachers believe that he should go to college next year. Mr. Gifford, Leo's chemistry teacher, has strongly advocated for Leo's early admission into college. He believes that this student has the potential to make a major contribution to medical science. Mrs. Robbins, Leo's guidance counselor, agrees. As an alumnus of the university that has offered the scholarship, Mrs. Robbins believes that this school is the best possible choice for Leo. When Leo's teachers have talked to Mr. and Mrs. Demchak regarding this recom-

mendation, they feel their opinions have been totally disregarded. It does not appear that the Demchaks had their son's best interests in mind when they made their decision against early graduation. Leo's teachers have mentioned the problem of Leo having finished all the courses that were suitable for him through a curriculum-compacting approach to instruction. The Demchaks responded, however, that they consider it to be the school's responsibility to provide him with whatever instruction he needs at whatever level is appropriate for his ability.

Background Information:

Leo has always been regarded as a highly creative thinker. His kindergarten teacher told his parents that she had never worked with a child who came up with so many interesting ideas and projects. When he was tested for the gifted program, the evaluation report indicated that Leo possessed "high levels of fluid ability." Other teachers have noted in their reports that his giftedness is characterized by a "quickness in thinking, intuition, and perception." Leo's academic record and teacher reports have always been exemplary.

Mr. and Mrs. Demchak understand, just as well as the teachers, how bright their son is, but they also

© 2005 by PRO-ED, Inc. All rights reserved. Duplicating this page is strictly prohibited.

feel he is too immature to go away to college, especially to a university in such a big city. They have a difficult time teaching him responsibility at home. It is hard for them to imagine what he would do away from home. Not too long ago, Leo got into trouble for vandalizing the community swimming pool. Last week, he came home drunk from a party. A couple of days ago, his mother found several marijuana cigarettes in his dresser drawer. And yesterday, his father caught him trying to crack the security code for the phone company on his computer. These are just a few examples of the problem behaviors that Leo has demonstrated since he started high school. Mr. and Mrs. Demchak understand that it is typical for adolescents to get in some trouble, and they are not overly concerned about these behaviors. However, they believe these behaviors indicate that Leo is not mature enough to live in an unsupervised setting. Mr. and Mrs. Demchak do not want to tell Leo's teachers about these incidents because they think this information may prejudice them against Leo. They want his teachers to continue to think of him in a very positive light.

Case Study Activities

Part I:
Role Playing

Break into groups of four or five students and assume one of the following roles: Mr. Demchak, Leo, Mr. Gifford, Mrs. Robbins, and Mrs. Demchak (an optional role). Simulate a conference in which the participants attempt to resolve this problem. Following the activity, write a summary of the resolution.

Resolution

_____

_____

_____

_____

_____

_____

_____

_____

_____

_____

_____

© 2005 by PRO-ED, Inc. All rights reserved. Duplicating this page is strictly prohibited.

Part II:
Individual or Group Case Analysis

Answer the following questions and be prepared to discuss them in class.

1. Do you think Leo's parents should let him accept the scholarship and go away to New York next year? Why or why not?

_____

_____

_____

_____

_____

_____

_____

2. Is there any relationship between Leo's problem behaviors and his intellectual profile? Explain your position.

_____

_____

_____

_____

_____

_____

_____

3. Should Mr. and Mrs. Demchak tell Leo's teachers about his behavior problems? Why or why not?

_____

_____

_____

_____

_____

_____

_____

© 2005 by PRO-ED, Inc. All rights reserved. Duplicating this page is strictly prohibited.

4. Should Mr. and Mrs. Demchak be seeking outside help for Leo's problems, or are these fairly normal behaviors that will probably diminish on their own if the Demchaks communicate their disapproval to their son on a regular basis? Explain your response.

_____

_____

_____

_____

_____

_____

5. If Leo stays at Carlton for the next 2 years, how can the school and his teachers accommodate his giftedness and provide him with an education that is motivating and challenging? How could technology be used to support a program of accelerated and enriched learning?

_____

_____

_____

_____

_____

_____

_____

6. Create A Question (optional)

_____

_____

_____

_____

_____

_____

_____

© 2005 by PRO-ED, Inc. All rights reserved. Duplicating this page is strictly prohibited.

CASE STUDIES

Lily

Lily is a 5-year-old kindergarten student at Kincaid Elementary School. She has been in school for only 2 weeks now, and she's having considerable difficulty adjusting. Lily is a very precocious child who is already reading on the second-grade level. She also demonstrates unusual abilities in the areas of art and problem solving. Her parents, Mr. and Mrs. Herrera, do not believe the school is providing her with the education she needs. Lily's teachers feel that all children need to learn basic rules regarding following directions and observing classroom procedures, regardless of the strengths they may also possess.

Ms. Gravier, Lily's art teacher, was initially delighted to have a student with such a high level of artistic ability in her class; however, she soon changed her mind. Lily never seemed to be interested in the art projects that Ms. Gravier had developed for the kindergartners. For example, if the art project of the day had to do with line drawings, it was Ms. Gravier's expectation that all of the children would engage in the line drawing activity. She did not tell them what to draw, she would merely specify the medium. According to Ms. Gravier, that type of assignment should allow for all students to express themselves as they saw fit. Frequently, Lily did not want to use the medium that Ms. Gravier had selected. She would refuse to participate and, in a petulant manner say, "I don't feel like markers today. I want to use watercolors." At first, Ms. Gravier tried to gently cajole her into completing the project of the day, but as Lily grew more resolute, Ms. Gravier became angry. She finally decided that if Lily refused to complete the specified project, she would sit in the corner and do nothing. Ms. Gravier felt that this was an appropriate consequence for the behavior in question.

Lily's kindergarten teacher, Mrs. Carson, is having problems with Lily as well. She simply will not follow the directions that are given in class or observe the basic classroom rules. For example, when Mrs. Carson starts the day, she has an opening time. At the end of this opening time, she explains the first instructional activity, which is also written on the schedule on the board. As soon as Mrs. Carson starts explaining what the students will be doing, Lily jumps up from the circle and begins the project. She has read the project on the board and figured out what to do, so she wants to start. Mrs. Carson will not allow her to start until all the children have the instructions. While Mrs. Carson is explaining the lesson to the other children, Lily sits there impatiently waiting, muttering things like, "This is stupid. Why do I have to wait?" As a consequence of this behavior, Mrs. Carson frequently makes Lily wait until everyone else has left the circle before she can begin. Sometimes, Mrs. Carson tells her to wait until 5 minutes after everyone else has started the project before she can begin. Lily is responsible for watching the clock so that she will know when she can start.

Another problem is that Lily will not raise her hand to answer questions, and she will not wait until Mrs. Carson gets the entire question out before answering. This is very annoying to Mrs. Carson, because none of the other children ever get a chance to listen to the question and try to figure out the answer. Lily also fails to stop working when Mrs. Carson tells the students to finish up and start another project. When Lily wants to continue on a project, she flatly tells Mrs. Carson that she is not going to stop until she is done. Mrs. Carson punishes her by withdrawing such privileges as free time or recess. Lily usually ends up crying. She does not really care about missing recess, but she does care that Mrs. Carson makes her spend the whole time sitting at her desk, studying spelling words that she knew when she was 4 years old.

Mr. and Mrs. Herrera are furious with the teachers and the principal. They are appalled that there are no gifted programs available until the third grade in this school district. They have asked the principal, Mr. Evans, to intervene. His suggestion is that they should pull Lily out for the year and start her again next year when she is more mature. Mrs. Carson thinks that Lily should be referred for a special education evaluation for behavioral problems.

Background Information:

Lily is the only child of Mr. and Mrs. Herrera, both of whom are doctors. Lily's precociousness has been a source of extreme pride for this family. They will

© 2005 by PRO-ED, Inc. All rights reserved. Duplicating this page is strictly prohibited.

readily admit that they have indulged her, perhaps a little more than they should, because they believe that she needs more flexibility because of her brightness. When she was tested at the age of 3, her *Wechsler Preschool and Primary Scale of Intelligence* (WPPSI; Wechsler, 1967) Full Scale IQ was 145. At approximately the same time, they started her in an exclusive preschool. Lily had quite a few adjustment problems in this setting. Her teacher felt that she was prone to temper tantrums and that she was a very willful child. Finally, after numerous meetings with the school to try to resolve their differences, the Herreras decided to make a large donation to the school's computer lab. There were few problems thereafter.

Case Study Activity

Individual or Group Case Analysis

Answer the following questions and be prepared to discuss them in class.

1. Should Lily be referred for a special education evaluation for her behavior? Why or why not?

_____

_____

_____

_____

_____

_____

_____

_____

2. Should Lily be pulled out of kindergarten and started again next year? Why or why not?

_____

_____

_____

_____

_____

_____

_____

© 2005 by PRO-ED, Inc. All rights reserved. Duplicating this page is strictly prohibited.

CASE STUDIES

3. Do schools legally have to meet the educational needs of gifted children? Explain your response. Why do you think the district does not have any gifted programs for children who are in the primary grades?

_____

_____

_____

_____

_____

_____

_____

4. If you were Mrs. Carson, how would you work with Lily to accommodate her learning needs and decrease her behavioral problems?

_____

_____

_____

_____

_____

_____

_____

5. Is it an appropriate strategy for Ms. Gravier to exclude Lily from art activities if she refuses to do what the rest of the class is doing? Why or why not? If you were Ms. Gravier, how would you work with this child?

_____

_____

_____

_____

_____

_____

_____

© 2005 by PRO-ED, Inc. All rights reserved. Duplicating this page is strictly prohibited.

6. Create A Question (optional)

_____

_____

_____

_____

_____

_____

_____

_____

Arletha

Arletha is a 10-year-old fifth grader at Walters Elementary School. Her language arts teacher, Mrs. Abrams, is impressed with Arletha's ability to write short stories and plays. Mrs. Abrams was initially surprised when Arletha turned in her first couple of stories, because Arletha is not one of her better students. In fact, her grades are generally in the low C to high D range. It is Mrs. Abrams's opinion that Arletha's literary works are of such a high quality that she could benefit from the gifted program. However, when she referred Arletha for the gifted program, she was informed by Mrs. Obe, the program's teacher, that Arletha did not qualify. Mrs. Obe told Mrs. Abrams that Arletha's standardized achievement scores were reviewed and that she was also given the standard screening test, the *Raven's Progressive Matrices* (Raven, Court, & Raven, 1986), for admission into the program. Arletha's achievement scores ranged from the 15th percentile in math to the 50th percentile in reading comprehension. Her composite score on the *Raven's* was at the 25th percentile. Mrs. Obe made it clear to Mrs. Abrams that Arletha's scores were well below that which is required for entrance into the school district's gifted and talented program.

Mrs. Abrams accepted Mrs. Obe's assessment of Arletha and became resigned to the fact that she must have been wrong about Arletha's talent. Two months later, Arletha turned in a notebook of haiku poetry for an assignment. Mrs. Abrams was astounded at the brilliance of Arletha's work. She took the notebook to Mrs. Obe's room and asked her to review Arletha's poetry and reconsider Arletha for the gifted and talented program at the school. Mrs. Obe casually glanced through the poems and replied that they were nice, but irrelevant. According to school district standards, only achievement scores and the results of the *Raven's* could be considered. Mrs. Abrams then asked her if that type of measurement was a fair assessment for an African American child like Arletha. Mrs. Obe laughed and said, "Well, she's an American, isn't she?

© 2005 by PRO-ED, Inc. All rights reserved. Duplicating this page is strictly prohibited.

CASE STUDIES

Of course, it's fair, especially the *Raven's,* which requires only puzzle-solving skills without language. It's one of the most culturally fair tests there is."

Background Information:

Arletha lives with a foster family. It is the fourth foster family with which she has lived since social services took her away from her parents who are drug addicts. As soon as Arletha entered a Headstart preschool at the age of 3, her teachers started filling out reports regarding neglect. These continued for 3 years until social services took Arletha and her brothers and placed them in different foster homes. Arletha was sexually abused by her first foster family when she was in first grade. Her second foster family kept her for 3 months, then the mother found out she was pregnant and became too tired to care for her. The next foster family abruptly left the state after caring for her for 8 months. Before Arletha was placed with the fourth foster family, social services evaluated her as being a depressed child who was in need of counseling. However, no one followed up on that recommendation.

Case Study Activity

Individual or Group Case Analysis

Answer the following questions and be prepared to discuss them in class.

1. How is it possible that Arletha's achievement scores are so low, yet her creative writing is exceptional? Does this mean that the achievement test is invalid?

_____

_____

_____

_____

_____

_____

2. Do you agree with Mrs. Obe's remarks about the fairness of the tests that are used for screening for the gifted and talented program? Should the fact that Arletha is an African American child have anything to do with her assessment for the gifted and talented program? Are there any other factors in this case that should be considered in assessing this child's potential?

_____

_____

_____

_____

_____

© 2005 by PRO-ED, Inc. All rights reserved. Duplicating this page is strictly prohibited.

3. Do you think Arletha is gifted? If so, should Mrs. Abrams persist in trying to get Arletha into the gifted program, or should Mrs. Abrams try to adjust her own instructional program to better meet Arletha's needs?

_____

_____

_____

_____

_____

_____

_____

4. Describe how Mrs. Abrams could modify the curriculum so that Arletha could fulfill her potential in creative writing. Give five possible strategies.

_____

_____

_____

_____

_____

_____

_____

_____

5. Do you think that entrance requirements to gifted and talented programs should be so high that the program is reserved for a select few who can best benefit from it, or should requirements be flexible enough to consider many different variables that affect a child's performance? Support your answer.

_____

_____

_____

_____

_____

_____

© 2005 by PRO-ED, Inc. All rights reserved. Duplicating this page is strictly prohibited.

6. Create A Question (optional)

_____

_____

_____

_____

_____

_____

_____

_____

Margo

Margo is a 14-year-old freshman at Peninsula High School. She was identified as gifted at the age of 8. The school district provided an excellent program of enrichment, allowing Margo the opportunity to pursue many interests. Margo is accomplished in many areas. She plays first flute with the school band, and she has won many prizes for both her ice skating and dance. Academically, she is above most of her peers in all areas, but she shows the greatest potential in science and math. Her hobbies include poetry writing and painting. Margo has a tremendous amount of energy and has been able to enjoy all of these activities in the past without experiencing stress. This year appears to be different.

Since she has started high school, Margo has begun to feel pressure from her parents, teachers, and friends regarding the amount of time she should be spending on certain activities. The school year started 3 weeks ago, and already Margo has been asked to make certain commitments that would preclude other activities that she has previously enjoyed. For example, her father has told her that he wants the science fair to be her number one priority for this school year. Her speech teacher has asked her to represent the school on the debate team, and her band teacher has asked her to compete as a soloist as well as a member

of a trio for the state band contest. Her ice skating coach expects her to train for a minimum of 2 hours per day so that she has a chance at the Metro Ice Competition in the spring, and her dance teacher expects her to be involved in four dance numbers at the spring recital as well as perform at numerous other fundraisers during the year.

Because Margo genuinely enjoys all of her activities, she has not chosen to drop out of any of them. However, she has not been able to arrange her schedule so that she can keep up with all the obligations to which she has committed herself. Margo is starting to miss certain obligations, causing her coaches, peers, parents, and teachers to become angry with her. For example, Margo was half an hour late for dance rehearsal because her band teacher kept the trio late to discuss the upcoming competition. At the end of rehearsal, Margo's dance teacher had a stern talk with her about tardiness. This talk lasted so long that Margo would have been 30 minutes late for a debate team meeting, but it did not matter because she was crying too hard to go. By the time she had walked home, there was an angry message on the machine from a peer whom she considered to be a good friend. The message said something to the effect that if Margo did not take her commitment to the debate

© 2005 by PRO-ED, Inc. All rights reserved. Duplicating this page is strictly prohibited.

team seriously, then she should drop out and give her slot to someone more deserving and more willing to put the time into the team commitment.

Margo started crying again. When her mother came home, Margo told her about some of the pressure she was starting to feel this year. Mrs. Finister, Margo's mother, takes great pride in her daughter's accomplishments. She was very responsive to Margo's emotional state, but she offered no solution, only the encouragement that, "You can do it, sweetie, if you really put your mind to it." Margo continued to feel badly, so when her father came home, she tried to talk to him. He immediately offered her what he thought was a realistic solution. He told her to drop everything except the science fair—which is the activity in which Margo has the least interest of all. Mrs. Finister overheard the discussion and came rushing in from the kitchen to castigate Mr. Finister. "Just because you have limited interests, you should not try to force your daughter into the same restrictive mold!" she said. Her parents then embarked on a heated discussion as Margo slipped away, feeling that her presence was not needed.

The next morning, Margo's debate team coach, Mrs. Bricker, stopped her as she was coming through the school door. Mrs. Bricker started to reprimand her when she noticed that Margo was going to cry. Margo did not look very good this morning. She had not slept well, worrying that she had let her friends and teachers down and not knowing what to do to make things better. Margo and Mrs. Bricker went into her classroom where Margo tearfully explained how she was feeling.

Later, in the faculty lounge, Mrs. Bricker mentioned Margo's dilemma to a couple of other teachers. She was saying that she really had a lot of empathy for gifted children like Margo because they experienced quite a bit of stress associated with their multipotentiality. Several teachers overheard Mrs. Bricker's conversation and started making negative comments. One of these teachers sarcastically said, "Those poor kids, they have such a rough go of it—good at everything, what a miserable life!" Another teacher remarked, "The only ones who whine and complain more than the gifted kids are their parents." A third teacher emphatically confirmed, "Boy, isn't that the truth!"

Background Information:

During her daughter's preschool years, Margo's mother keenly observed Margo's special skills in a wide variety of areas. As a conscientious mother, Mrs. Finister went out of her way to make sure that Margo had the opportunities to explore her many talents. Mrs. Finister watched with amazement as Margo excelled in activity after activity. She never forced Margo into any activity. She didn't have to—Margo seemed to relish every opportunity to learn a new skill or activity. Occasionally, Mrs. Finister would think that Margo was involved with too many different activities. Then again, she also felt that Margo was so gifted that it was her responsibility to expose her to as many possibilities as she could and then let her decide what she wanted to continue later on in life. Mrs. Finister eventually got Margo involved in so many activities that she had to quit her job so that Margo could enjoy full participation. But the truth of the matter is that Mrs. Finister did not mind because she believed that her most important job was parenting Margo. She feels fortunate to have a daughter who is so talented.

© 2005 by PRO-ED, Inc. All rights reserved. Duplicating this page is strictly prohibited.

CASE STUDIES

Individual or Group Case Analysis

Answer the following questions and be prepared to discuss them in class.

1. Is it unusual for a gifted student to experience talent in such a wide range of areas? Margo did not seem to have any problems keeping up with all her activities in elementary and middle school. Why is she experiencing problems in high school?

_____

_____

_____

_____

_____

_____

2. What is your opinion of Mrs. Finister's attitude about Margo's activities? What do you think of Mr. Finister's attitude?

_____

_____

_____

_____

_____

_____

3. Do you think Margo is simply overreacting to her peer's comments about missing the debate team meeting, or do you think that she is experiencing significant stress? What might happen if Margo and her family do not resolve this problem?

_____

_____

_____

_____

_____

_____

© 2005 by PRO-ED, Inc. All rights reserved. Duplicating this page is strictly prohibited.

4. Why do you think those teachers in the faculty lounge had negative reactions to Mrs. Bricker's comments about gifted students and their parents? What do you think is the public's perception of gifted students? Do you think these perceptions influence funding for gifted programs?

_____

_____

_____

_____

_____

_____

_____

_____

5. Do gifted students typically have more stress than other students? How could Mrs. Bricker provide assistance to Margo?

_____

_____

_____

_____

_____

_____

_____

_____

6. Create A Question (optional)

_____

_____

_____

_____

_____

_____

_____

_____

© 2005 by PRO-ED, Inc. All rights reserved. Duplicating this page is strictly prohibited.

CASE STUDIES

ABOUT THE AUTHOR

Peggy L. Anderson is a professor and special education program coordinator in the Teacher Education Department at Metropolitan State College of Denver. She has taught students with mild to moderate needs at the elementary and middle school levels in South Carolina and Florida. Her master's degree is from the Citadel and her doctorate is from the University of Denver. She completed her postdoctoral work with the Department of Pediatrics at Johns Hopkins University. Her research has focused on language-learning disabilities, assessment, inclusion, and curriculum accessibility.